The KETO Soup Bowl

50 delicious fat-burning, health-boosting bowls of soup, chowder, hodgepodge, gumbo, stew, and gazpacho

CARRIE BROWN

from the Ketovangelist Kitchen

Text and Photography Copyright © 2017 Carrie Brown

All rights reserved.

No part of this publication may be reproduced, distributed, or transmitted in any form or by any means, including photocopying, recording, or other electronic or mechanical methods, without the prior written permission of the author.

Recipes are provided for private and personal use only.

The text and recipes should not be considered a substitute for professional medical advice. The author shall not be held liable for any adverse effects arising from the use of the information and recipes contained herein. The reader should consult a qualified medical professional before starting any new health or diet program.

ISBN-10: 1974503062
ISBN-13: 978-1974503063

DEDICATION

Marc Levine

I would not be here if not for you. My life would not look anything like it does now if not for your influence. You hold my feet to the fire in a way that no one else has ever been brave enough to do. You challenge me, you tell me when I am being ridiculous, and you tell me who I really am. I am who I am today because of your persistence and love.

No matter that we no longer see each other, you continue to be the most important thing for my mind and soul.

ACKNOWLEDGMENTS

Rekka Jay — for cover-creating sorcery, along with perfect proofing, outstanding cheerleading from the sidelines, and so much more I've lost track — you're The Best!

Nancy Crowell — for making me use my tripod, for taste-testing more soups in a week than you even thought was legal, for keeping Mr. McHenry entertained while I shot stuff, and for loving my Cheesy Biscuits almost as much as life itself.

The Soup Taste Test Crew — Nancy Crowell aka The Roomie, Alisen Petersen, Duane Blanchard, Mic Van Putten, Taylor Van Putten, Jonathan and Angela Bailor. Your endless enthusiasm for my soupy creations served only to raise my game and increase my excitement for all things vegetable even more.

Alisen Peterson Blanchard — for showing up with Thai food, movies, girl-time, and a good giggle when my book-writing mojo stalled.

Bala Silvakumar — I love how you make me look through your lens!

You — if you bought this book, follow my blog, or listen to our shows, you are the reason that I do what I do. Thank you for choosing the path to your health and wellness, and for being a part of my world.

Marc Levine — for all that, and a bit more.

CONTENTS

The Start of a Soup Kitchen 1

Soups Are Magical 3

Ingredients 7

Equipment 13

Soup How To 17

Servings Sizes and Macro Calculations 21

Recipes: Main Course Soups 23

Recipes: BYO (Build Your Own) Soups 75

Biscuits 103

Konjac Flour: What, Why, How 107

Ketovangelist Resources 108

Where to Find Me 109

Carrie Brown 110

Index 111

THE START OF A SOUP KITCHEN

For a girl who's more at home in the kitchen than just about anywhere else on earth; a girl regularly decked out in a chocolate and creamed spinach splattered apron; a girl who has been cooking – ok, well at least sifting flour and grating cheese – since she was 3 years old, I feel a little silly sharing this, but I believe in honesty, so here goes: the thought of making soups from scratch scared me for years. There. I typed it out loud. I realize this is a strange admission in the opening paragraph of a soup book, but it will all make sense in a paragraph or two. At least, that's the plan.

For my first 12 years or so on earth, whenever we ate soup at home it was invariably out of a packet – a dry powder mixed up with water and duly heated on the stove top until piping hot. I loved it when we had soup. I especially loved the tomato and chicken soups that we slurped – oh if only we had been allowed to slurp! – down. The thicker, creamier soup offerings were always welcome in my belly. I didn't care for the clear vegetable soups much, with their thin, pale, golden liquid and re-hydrated confetti of vegetable pieces bobbing around on top, although I always ate them. In our house you ate everything that was ever put in front of you. Those were the rules.

Having grown up thinking that soup was produced by mixing a special powder and water together, I suppose it is no great surprise that my young mind could not fathom how it was even possible to create soup from real food. I concluded that soup production from things that used to be alive and kicking had to be a terribly complicated business. I just couldn't imagine how vegetables could be teased into something thick, comforting, or tasty if it didn't involve a magic powder. The 12-year-old Carrie concluded, therefore, that there must be a spot of wizardry required in soup-making, because packet soup is definitely wizardry. And if you were going to make soup without the aid of packet wizardry, it must mean that you were *really* clever.

I ate stacks of packet soups in those formative years.

At some point in my early teens my mother started to make Cucumber Soup from scratch, thanks to an enormous and ongoing cucumber harvest courtesy of my father and his trusty greenhouse. It seemed like he lived in that greenhouse at times. Seeds would go in – dressed in colorful little packets – and copious amounts of salad vegetables would later come marching out. He grew all manner of things, but that man really knew how to raise a fantastic cucumber.

Cucumber Soup was my mother's answer to the deluge of cucumbers threatening to bury her alive in our kitchen. Despite having eaten gallon upon gallon of my mother's pale green concoction over the years, I have no idea how she made it. In my mind it had to be an intrinsically magical method. It was soup, after all. Wizardry must have been involved.

In my early twenties I graduated to canned soup – I expect while I was living the time-and-money-starved student life in London – when cream-of-anything soups became a staple. There was still no correlation between soup and real food though. Canned soups with their ridiculously smooth, thick, and gloopy consistencies seemed even more magical than rehydrated powders. Given the evidence, I continued to believe that soup made from scratch was a mythical creature found only in fancy restaurants with extraordinarily clever chefs doing magic behind the curtain. All a bit Wizard of Oz if you ask me. It just never occurred to me to try and make any soup myself.

Then, one morning, after I got my first mortgage and moved into my condo (flat) with a kitchen so small you could touch two opposite walls at the same time, I had a very wild hare and made Leek and Potato Soup. I don't know what came over me; or what inspired me. I didn't know what I was doing, either. I just waded right on into Soup Land and winged it. Threw a large handfuls of sautéed leeks into some chicken stock with a slab of butter, and then added a big old pile of mashed potatoes. It was *the bomb*. I instantly became soup obsessed. Nothing has ever floated my boat quite like that first bowlful of homemade Leek and Potato Soup. I can still taste it now.

After gallons of Leek and Potato soup spurred both my confidence and my imagination, I started making soup out of anything that sat still long enough. Beets (beetroot) featured heavily, as I recall. There was often a Tupperware tub of thick, brilliantly colored purpleness lolling in the corner of my 'fridge.

The "recipes" were easy, earthy, entirely uncomplicated, and always made up on the spur of the moment – never to be replicated because I never wrote them down. Thickened by just the vegetables themselves, and usually pimped out with nothing more than a dollop of dairy – a spoonful of cream here, a knob of butter there – soups rapidly became my signature dish and go-to comfort food. I dished them up for lunch, and I served them up for dinner – their dazzling colors brightening many a dull winter evening. Friends gazed cautiously at the pale yet gaudy green of my Leek and Potato Soup before becoming converted at the third spoonful.

From packets of powder wizardry to this book's all-KETO-all-the-time creations, soups have always featured heavily in my life. Little did I know that one of my biggest culinary fears would turn out to be the subject of my second cookbook. Funny how things like that happen in life.

So if one of your fears is how to eat KETO – and / or how to include veggies in your KETO life without resorting to choking down a pile of soggy greens – this is the cookbook for you. You will learn how to turn humble KETO ingredients into something quite fantastic. Go on! Embrace your fears!

Once you do, you too will realize that soups are magical.

www.carriebrown.com

SOUPS ARE MAGICAL

It turns out that despite my dodgy childhood logic, and for entirely different reasons, I was right. Soup IS magical. Wait, let me clarify that just a tad. *Some* soups are magical. The powdered and canned soups of my youth no longer qualify for this revered title. And while I can't speak for all made-from-scratch soups in the world, I can say with certainty that the soups in this book are all kinds of magical. What is it that makes them so? Veggies. The magic is all in the veggies.

Wait. What? But KETO isn't about veggies! It's all about the meat! And the healthy fats! Right. But when it comes to soups – if you think about your favorite ones – they mostly revolve around the carbs. All the carbs! Pasta, potatoes, carrots, peas, dumplings, noodles, rice, tortillas…and on and on with the carbage.

And that's where the non-starchy veggies come in. They make it possible for you to get all your favorites – only KETOfied. Veggies allow a huge amount of variety into your culinary world, and lack of variety is something that many Keto-ers struggle with. I'm all for anything that helps people stay on the KETO path.

And there's more! For everyone keen on reaching their optimal health and body-fat goals, non-starchy veggies can help. Notwithstanding that our bodies need excellent sources of protein and healthy fats to thrive, non-starchy vegetables will give you added micronutrients, fiber, and water. And that, is pretty much all I am going to say on the subject of nutrition because this is a cookbook to help you get more nutrition inside you – as deliciously as possible – not a book to explain the ins and outs of the nutrition itself. This book will help you with the how, because the how is what we need out here in the time-and-budget-challenged real world.

Right after the publication of my fat-burning, health-boosting ice-cream cookbook – The KETO Ice Cream Scoop – I asked readers what kinds of recipes they wanted me to focus on next. The answers were resounding: "Help us eat more veggies!", "Make vegetables delicious!", and "New ways to eat veggies, please!"

So here's a cookbook filled with 50 delicious new ways to KETO while dialing up your non-starchy veggie intake. Maybe I should have titled it "How To Eat Vegetables Without Even Realizing It".

Here's why these soups are magical:

- **They are wildly nutritious.** Proteins, healthy fats, and non-starchy veggies. These recipes are all KETO all the time, although your taste buds won't believe it. There is no better way to get a ton of real, whole food goodness into your body. We love non-starchy veggies for the variety they bring to the proceedings!

- **You can eat more veggies in soup form before you get full than if they were in whole form.** If one of your goals is to cram more nutrition into your day, soups do it for you; not to mention that with soups you don't feel like you've been munching on veggies all day long. You just feel like you've been slurping down deliciousness.

- **They don't look like vegetables.** If you – or those you feed – are not typically of the vegetable persuasion, this could well be the all-star game-changer. Our minds are great trick players – if it tastes great and doesn't look like something you thought you didn't like, it's a slam dunk. Top tip: ask people if they like it before you tell 'em what's in it.

- **They don't taste like vegetables.** At least they don't taste like the vegetables you've been used to. With these soups you can eat things that you don't like in real life. Cabbage that tastes like tortilla soup? Brussels Sprouts that taste like bacon? Cauliflower that tastes like rich cheese sauce? Yes! Please! And can I have seconds?

- **They are simple and easy to make.** Simple recipes that come together in a heartbeat and are easy enough for kitchen novices. Just learning your way around a kitchen? Start with soups!

- **They are low maintenance.** You can wander off and do something else while they are cooking. Dishes? Done. Laundry folded? Done. Quick break with a cuppa? Done.

- **They can easily be made in large batches.** It takes almost no more time to make 16 servings than it does 4. Make a huge pot and enjoy effort-free meals for several days.

- **They are freezable.** Make large batches, freeze in portion-sized containers, and you have instant meals at your fingertips; except these instant meals are healthier than just about anything else on earth that you could eat.

- **They are easily portable.** Perfect for lunches, road trips or any time you need to have a tasty, nutritious meal on the go.

- **They are fast and easy to reheat.** A pan on the stovetop or a quick spin in the microwave, soups are reheated and ready to go in minutes.

- **They are just as tasty cold as they are hot.** Well, most of them. Some soups just need to be hot to make sense – like Chili – but others are equally as delicious cold. Soups aren't just for winter anymore.

- **They only need a spoon to eat them.** Then, if finding a spoon is an issue, you can just drink them.

Be brave! Be wild!

Buy non-starchy veggies that are new to you. Never eaten leeks? Check out the Salmon and Leek Chowder. Buy non-starchy veggies that you always thought you didn't like. Don't care for cauliflower? The Cauliflower Cheese Soup will surely change your mind. Fennel never had you at hello? The Sausage, Leek and Fennel Soup makes a great introduction to this delicious bulb. Celery has never really wowed me in real life, but combining it with sage and making it creamy turned it into an all-time winner for me. Green beans are not my favorite, but when I added them to a creamy bowl of sautéed onions and mushrooms I was all over those babies.

I think these soup recipes will surprise you. I think you'll find you can eat and enjoy more veggies than you ever thought possible.

Because soups are magical. Soups *rock*.

First, before we get cooking, we'll run through the ingredients that you will need, we'll take a peek at the equipment you'll use, and then we'll do a down-and-dirty Soup Making 101.

If you read these three (short!) sections first, your soup making will get off to a flying start.

And lastly, just one teensy-weensy word of caution before you dive headlong into the minutiae of soup-making and then sprint to the kitchen. If you are not used to eating loads of veggies, can I suggest that a slower and more gentle approach may be appropriate? Veggies are awesome, but your inner workings would likely appreciate a gradual increase in all that fabulous dietary fiber as opposed to a full-on floodgate being opened. Otherwise you may be forced to spend a day or two sleeping on the couch and / or not straying too far from the bathroom. Don't ask me how I know.

Now let's get this soup show on the road!

~~~~~~

There follows chapters that cover the main ingredients and equipment that I use to create these delicious recipes.

For more info on the ingredients and equipment that I use and love in my KETO kitchen, just head to the web addresses below:

INGREDIENTS: http://carriebrown.com/archives/23109

EQUIPMENT: http://carriebrown.com/archives/23310

www.carriebrown.com

INGREDIENTS

Given that one of my life focuses these days is to help you squeeze non-starchy veggies – as deliciously as possible – into your KETO day, it will come as no surprise to you that there's a bunch of veggies involved in the ingredients list. Which is entirely as it should be – but you'll also find a smattering of other bits and bobs thrown in to help you transform those magnificent veggies into enticing bowls of liquid scrumptiousness.

Here – in alphabetical order – is a quick guide to all those other bits and bobs. Some of them may be new to you – but don't panic! Once you've tried a few of the recipes out, those bits and bobs will become old, faithful friends. You may even wonder how you lived without them in your pantry up until now.

But first, let's just talk about the star performers for a minute.

A lot of the ingredients in this book are simply fabulous, fresh vegetables. You will be amazed at how you are able to tease these humble stalwarts of the produce department into fantastically flavored bowls of smooth and creamy deliciousness, with only a dash of this and a pinch of that to turn them from ordinary into miraculous.

Whether you buy your veggies from a local farmers market, a neighborhood co-op, or the grocery store, always buy the freshest produce that you can find, and use it as soon as possible.

When shopping for a recipe, note that the weight of the vegetables in the recipe is the amount of the vegetable that you actually use. It does not include all the roots and leaves and trimmings. If it says 1 lb. of cauliflower it means 1 lb. of white florets, not a whole cauliflower that weighed 1 lb. including all the outer leaves and stalks. So when you are weighing your veggies at the store allow some extra weight for the unusable parts that you will discard. I did it this way because each vegetable will have a different amount of unusable parts, so giving you the weight of veggies that you will actually use is by far the most accurate way to ensure that your soup is a roaring success.

Now let's take a quick look at the other things that you'll need.

<u>Avocado Oil</u>

Avocado oil is virtually tasteless, liquid at room temperature, and has a very high smoke point – meaning that you can use it for all sorts of heated applications without it degrading or becoming unstable. Also, it comes from avocados, and I suspect there's nothing more I need to say here.

<u>Butter</u>

Ah, butter. Of course there's butter involved in these recipes, and when there is some called for I highly recommend using butter from grass-fed cows, produced without the use of hormones or antibiotics. I use Kerrygold Irish Butter in my recipes. It's awesome and it reminds me of my homeland. I'm British, it's close enough.

You can swap out the butter for coconut oil if you need dairy-free or vegan options.

Coconut Milk

Thick – this is full-fat, very thick, comes in a can, and solidifies in the 'fridge. It is sometimes called coconut cream. It is made from coconut meat, and is very high in very healthy fats, especially MCTs (Medium Chain Triglycerides). I won't bore you with the technical details of MCTs – just know that they are extremely good for you. Thick coconut milk helps create a smooth and creamy texture. You can use thick coconut milk to replace the heavy (double) cream in these recipes if you want or need dairy-free or vegan versions.

Make sure that you buy it unsweetened, and shake the can very well before you open it. You can find it in most grocery stores and it is often located with the Asian and / or Indian foods. I used Thai Kitchen Unsweetened Coconut Milk for the recipes in this book.

Thin – this comes in a carton and is thin like cow's milk, but is very white. It does not become thick when cold. Make sure that you buy it unsweetened. I used Trader Joe's Unsweetened Coconut Milk Beverage for the recipes in this book that call for it.

In a pinch you can use them interchangeably in these recipes if you have one type on hand and not the other. The flavor and consistency of the final soup will be different to that intended, but nothing *terrible* will happen. If you have thick and need thin, you could dilute some thick with water to give a thinner consistency and reduce the richness. If you have thin and need thick, you'll end up with a thinner soup with less body to it. The world won't end.

Coconut Oil

Coconut oil is not only one of the healthiest oils there is, it is also extremely stable when heated. This is why it is one of my oils of choice when sautéing, or otherwise needing to heat an oil. It is a solid at room temperature, but melts very easily when the smallest amount of heat is applied, or when it's summer.

Different brands have varying degrees of coconut flavor, from none at all to a definite coconutty undertone. Find the brand you like and then never look back.

I used Trader Joe's Coconut Oil for these recipes because it has no coconut flavor at all once cooked. Call me strange but I didn't want every soup to taste like coconut.

Guar gum

Veggies are made up of, in large part, water and fiber – not things that mix together terribly well once they are liquidized. The two parts have a tendency to separate out over time – not terribly attractive and not terribly tasty either. To fix this we need something to make them stick together better, and to help make a very smooth and creamy emulsion. A little something to improve the texture of the finished soup. Enter guar gum.

Guar gum is made from ground guar beans and is an emulsifier and thickener. It also has magical powers in the suspension department. Wondering how those beefy mushroom pieces stay evenly suspended throughout the creamy soup base instead of crashing down to languish on the bottom? Guar gum. Guar gum is our friend.

A little bit of guar gum goes a very long way, so don't let the price scare you. One packet will last you a very long time. More is not better when it comes to guar gum – use only what the recipe states.

When using guar gum be careful not to over blend the soup once you have added it – you don't want a fluffy, aerated soup, and neither do you want a gluey one. Add it right at the end and then only blend for 5 seconds.

Guar gum is readily available online and increasingly available in grocery stores. Store guar gum in an air-tight jar. I used Bob's Red Mill brand guar gum in these recipes.

Herbs

Like spices, herbs can have a completely transformative effect on the flavor of soups. Herbs are little powerhouses in the flavor department of life. Beet Soup is tasty, but add a bunch of tarragon and your taste buds will enter a whole new level of awesome. Don't leave the herbs out because you think herbs are small and insignificant. Herbs are important, lovely readers!

If you're wondering about fresh v. dry when it comes to herbs, here's a few things to keep in mind:

- They don't taste the same. For example, soups flavored with dried sage will taste different to soups flavored with fresh sage.

- Dry herbs are much more potent than fresh herbs. If you need to swap out dry for fresh or vice versa, do so in the ratio of 1:3 – that is you will need 3 times the amount of fresh herbs to get the same potency as that of dry. 1 teaspoon dry = 3 teaspoons fresh.

- Dry herbs should be added at the start of cooking, fresh herbs towards the end. Here's why – dry herbs are more robust, fresh more delicate. Dry can withstand the extra heat and cooking time whereas fresh will lose some of their flavor. Dry herbs also need more time for their flavors to be released, whereas fresh give up their flavor readily.

- Dry herbs are way more expensive than home-grown fresh herbs, whereas store-bought fresh herbs are the most expensive of them all.

This year I got annoyed enough by the price of store-bought fresh herbs that I started a little herb garden at the Ketovangelist Kitchen. Not only was it fun to see stuff grow, and oh-so-handy having a never-ending supply of fresh herbs right outside my kitchen door, but it saved me a veritable fortune. Each herb start cost me $1.25 – less than half the price of just a couple of sprigs of fresh herbs from the store – and those starts kept me in herbs for the entire season.

Top tip #1: I planted the herb starts in pots so that they were contained and didn't overrun the entire garden.

Top tip #2: Want your herb garden on steroids? Water them with coffee grounds. Herb rambunctiousness will abound in your garden. You have been warned.

When I do buy dried herbs – a girl can't grow every herb on earth on her terrace – I buy small quantities from a store that sells them loose. Buying loose herbs is so much cheaper than buying them pre-packaged a) because you don't have to buy more than you need, b) there is less chance that they will lose their flavor before you use them, and c) you won't be buying glass containers over and over again. You also don't know how long those jars have sat there. Loose dried herbs tend to get turned over much quicker. Which means they're fresher. Fresher dried herbs. We love that.

Heavy Cream (Double Cream outside of the US)

I use heavy cream in many of these soups because 1. Duh, KETO and 2. It imparts a particularly smooth and creamy result, as well as an extra depth of flavor. I do love the odd splash (or 10) of cream here and there.

I recommend that you buy cream that has no added ingredients. If you can find organic cream with no hormones or antibiotics, that is produced by grass-fed cows, so much the better.

Look for heavy cream that does not say UHT on the carton. UHT cream has been treated at very high temperatures to give it a long shelf-life, but that heating also destroys the flavor. I never really understood why cream would need a long shelf-life. If it gets as far as my 'fridge, it won't be there on the shelf for long.

If you need to make a recipe dairy-free or vegan, replace the heavy cream with thick coconut milk. The taste and texture will not be the same, but it will be close.

Konjac Flour (Glucomannan Powder)

I use konjac flour – also known as glucomannan powder – to replace cornstarch or flour as a thickener. It is a soluble plant fiber that thickens with 10x the power of cornstarch, so a little goes a very long way. It is tasteless, easy to use, and can be used in all sorts of cooking applications for thickening and gelling. Konjac flour is awesome. I thoroughly encourage you to make friends with it and keep some stocked in your pantry. You'll find a whole bunch of other recipes that use konjac flour over at www.carriebrown.com. Like Cheese Sauce. Hello.

See page 107 for an entire rundown of why you cannot go another day without a container of konjac flour in your KETO pantry. One tub will last you a really long time. Also, you'll love me after the first time you use it. Or the second. But probably the first.

Konjac flour is readily available online or in stores that sell supplements.

Sea salt

Salt is used to brighten and intensify the flavors of the vegetables in soups – which often get a whole lot less powerful once they are cooked. Sea salt stops them from tasting flat. I highly recommend using coarse sea salt instead of regular table salt. Sea salt has an improved flavor, and a higher concentration of minerals than regular table salt.

I also recommend measuring the sea salt per the amount called for in the recipe. While salty soup is not a disaster, the right amount of salt will rock your taste buds. I suggest you add per the recipe and then adjust with more if you feel it needs it. Then add just a little at a time.

Spices

Spices are awesome. They can perk up the most ordinary of dishes into something rather swoon-worthy. The day I decided – on a whim – to add Chinese Five Spice to my Cauliflower Soup it ended up going down as a red letter day in the Brown household. Who knew that a dash of reddish-brown powder could make cauliflower one of the cool kids on the vegetable block?

I typically buy my spices in small amounts, as I need them, from a store that sells them loose, rather than buying pre-packaged jars that I may not use up before they go stale and lose their potency. Spices sold in jars are also significantly more expensive than buying loose. Store your spices in air-tight glass containers, and keep them in a cool, dark place. Heat and sunlight will adversely affect the flavor and potency of the spices. You're welcome.

Stock

Stock forms the basis of the majority of the soups in this cookbook. Well, apart from the veggies that is.

If you have the time, energy, money, an endless source of carcasses and bones, and the inclination, go ahead and make your own stock. Homemade stock has a richness and body that you really can't compare with boxed stock. When I'm in my 80's I'll definitely be making my own, but for the here and now – filled with all the things that life throws our way – I'm happy to leave the stock-making up to (Trader) Joe. Joe makes good stock.

Find the best stock that you can, where best = reading the label and keeping a beady eye out for sugars of any kind, ingredients made of grains, and artificial anything. You don't want or need any of those in your stock. It's amazing what manufacturers throw in their wares these days. Stock should be meat, water, veggies, and a few seasonings thrown in for good measure. Except for vegetable stock – there shouldn't be any meat in that. Just saying.

You may also opt to use stock cubes and water instead of ready-made boxed stock. All I'll caution you with is – read the label. It's pretty wild what they can cram into a tiny cube, and not all of it good.

I used Trader Joe's chicken, beef, and vegetable stocks for the recipes in this book. It's cheap, organic, and filled with all good things. Just like good stock should be.

Xanthan Gum

You'll need to get yourself some xanthan gum if you're planning on making any of the delicious biscuit / scone recipes at the back of this cookbook.

Xanthan gum is a thickener and it also strengthens the structure of the biscuit – traditionally achieved with the gluten in flour. Using almond flour instead of flours made from grains give a softer, more fragile texture and less lift. Xanthan gum helps with that. It also improves the texture of your biscuits. You only need a very small, but important, amount.

For more uses for xanthan gum, head over to www.carriebrown.com, and click on the recipes link where you'll find all sorts of fantastical recipes that use it. We love xanthan gum.

Xanthan gum is readily available online and increasingly available in grocery stores. Store xanthan gum in an air-tight jar. I used Bob's Red Mill brand xanthan gum in these recipes.

www.carriebrown.com

EQUIPMENT

In the equipment department, there's really only two things you *need* for great soup – a large pan and a blender. Everything else just makes life easier and faster.

Here's a list of the things that I employ when I am in full-on soup mode. Which is often.

Stock Pots / Pans

I use Le Creuset pans. They're cast-iron, heavy as all get out, wildly expensive, and come in a fantastic range of colors – which means they're pretty. They will also last you a lifetime, although I have witnessed one breaking clean in half when it was dropped on a tile floor.

You do not need Le Creuset pans to make great soup. I am not going to get into the whys and wherefores of cast iron v. the rest, but I'll just say that if you cook a lot and have a budget for Le Creuset, get them. If not, use what you have. If you're in the market for new pans, get the best you can that fits your budget. Making great soup does not need to bankrupt you.

Whatever brand of pans you use, I thoroughly recommend getting a stock pot if you are going to make any amount of soup. They make large batches a breeze. I have a 16 quart stock pot and another one so large I am planning on using it as the fall-out shelter in an emergency.

Some veggies – especially green leafy ones – start off all big and brave and then promptly collapse into a soft and mushy heap once a modicum of heat is applied. This is where stock pots come into their own. I can cram 4 lbs. of spinach into my stock pot in one go; a regular saucepan could never even hope to handle that amount of greenery.

I love my stock pots. Soup making would be a whole lot messier and take a whole lot longer without them.

High Powered Blender OR Blender OR Food processor

A Vitamix will be your very best friend for fantastic soups. Smooth, smooth, smooth. And then a bit smoother. These machines smash everything that goes in them into liquid. There's a few exceptions to that last statement, but none that you'll encounter in these recipes. High powered blenders are amazing. I even take mine on vacation with me, as long as it doesn't involve flying on a plane. I can't even imagine explaining that one to the TSA. They'd see that as ample cause for a pat-down right there.

I also have a second jug for my Vitamix – I find having a second blending container incredibly handy. Or maybe I just don't like washing up when I am on a roll in the kitchen. A second jug is especially convenient when there's a soup-making marathon under way. I am all about getting the most done in the least time. A second jug helps with that.

I have a Kitchen Aid 5-speed blender in addition to my Vitamix for those times when I don't want to pulverize everything into oblivion. Some things don't require the extra power. I use my regular blender when I don't want or need to use the Vitamix. However, I always pick the high-speed blender over the regular blender for making soups.

If a regular blender is what you have, use that. If you are in the market for a new blender, and have the budget, get a high-speed blender – you will not regret it.

I also have a Cuisinart Elite 14-cup Food Processor. It comes with three bowls that sit inside one another so you can do three different things before you have to wash up, and I love that. It also has a large capacity, which would be very useful if I needed to use it for making large batches of soup. If you don't have a blender but have a food processor you can still make soups.

Weighing Scale

There is only one way to get accurate, consistent, fantastic results every single time you make a recipe, and that is to weigh your non-liquid ingredients. Cups are handy, and super useful for liquids, but they are just not accurate enough for consistent results when dealing with solid ingredients. Worse still, when it comes to vegetables we tend to eyeball it, but a large cauliflower in England is an entirely different entity to a large cauliflower in America, whereas a weight is a weight wherever you are. I weigh everything. Every time.

The scale I use has a flat weighing plate, a pull-out digital display, and weighs in both metric and imperial. It also has the ability to zero out what is on the display so you can weigh directly into the container, bowl or blender jug of your choice, which means less work and less dirty dishes. We love that.

If you don't have a kitchen scale, please avail yourself of one. Trade in your bathroom scale for one, put one on your Christmas list, bat your eyes at your spouse, or barter your homegrown lettuces in exchange for one. Just get one. Please. Thank you.

Knives

A good set of sharp knives will make processing large quantities of veggies much easier. I still use the set of knives I had when I was studying at the National Bakery School in London. That's what I mean by a good set – they will last a lifetime. A quick sharpen on the steel every month and they're good to go for any number of fun slicing activities. These knives are workhorses.

My knives are Victorinox – makers of the original Swiss army knife. They're expensive, but if you're cooking a lot, the cost per use plummets when you take into account that you will never need to replace them.

Apart from all the practicalities, they just make cooking more pleasurable.

Ladles

This may seem obvious, but I thought I'd mention it anyway. In the midst of soup production, the very best thing to get your veggies out of the pan and into the blender is a ladle. Scooping the hot veggies out of the hot pan with a tool design especially for that purpose is just the cleanest and most-splash proof method. It's also the safest.

And the best thing to serve your scrumptious soup with is, yes, also a ladle. Of all the tools that hang down from under my kitchen cabinets, the ladle is the most used.

Melamine Pouring Bowls

I have lots of these bowls. They're light, and they have handles and spouts. They are the perfect solution for soups because you can use them as holding vessels when you are processing large batches. The spouts and handles make it easy to transfer soup back into the pan when all the batches have been processed. If that last line totally didn't make sense, it will once you read the chapter "Soup How To".

Melamine means they do not transfer flavors and colors like plastics do, but they are way lighter than glass. They even stack neatly when not in use.

Spatulas

You can never have too many flexible spatulas lying around when you're in the middle of soup making. Rubber is good, as is silicone. Smooth and super flexible is the kind of spatulas we are after. Great for getting all the soup out of the blender, the pan, and just about anything else.

Sieves

I am a perfectionist, so I use sieves a lot. I'll sieve anything that sits still long enough, given the opportunity. In my little world, texture perfection is mandatory, so sieving is important.

With soups, however, I mostly let the high-speed blender do all the hard work. You can live without a sieve for most of these soup recipes, although if asparagus is on your soup-making list I strongly encourage you to avail yourself of at least one fine mesh sieve, unless you enjoy eating soup that feels like it has several pieces of hair floating in it. Waiter! There's a hair in my soup!

Pyrex Glass Storage

In the Brown house, when it comes to food storage, it's got to be glass. Specifically, I use Pyrex 7-cup round dishes or ½ gallon Mason Jars for storing my soups in the 'fridge and freezer.

I have never been a fan of plastic for food storage. If plastic is capable of absorbing colors and flavors, it follows that the plastic is not impermeable. The thought that the chemicals in plastic are merrily transferring themselves back into my soups is highly unpleasant to me. Glass it is.

Immersion Blender

I have an immersion blender which I use for giving defrosted soups a quick whizz to return their texture to its former creamy awesomeness. Due to the high water content of veggies, and because these soups are not full of chemical junk, some of them separate when they defrost. All they need is a quick blend to emulsify them again. I either give them a fast spin in the blender, or use an immersion blender right there in the bowl or pan. If you don't have an immersion blender, use your blender. The immersion blender just saves you washing the blender jug up. I do like not having to wash the blender jug up.

Other Equipment

I also have on hand:

- Chopping boards
- Measuring cups (for liquids)
- Measuring spoons (for spices, herbs, guar gum, etc.)
- Microplanes (for zesting)
- Whisks – small, medium, large

~~~~~~

Some KETO Soup Bowl love:

"Thanks Carrie! I love Potato and Leek soup, but you know what, I think I love Cauliflower and Leek soup even more! My second batch is on the stove cooking, and leeks are becoming a staple in my house now!" ~ Jenny

"Carrie has put together the most amazing collection of soups that you will ever try. There's definitely a soup here for everyone. Healthy and creamy soups – pages and pages of soups that will fill your tummy, satisfy your taste buds and even trim your waistline at the same time. Without a doubt, my two favorites are the Chicken and Mushroom Soup and the Creamed Onion Soup. This book is a must have for everyone's cookbook collection – especially if you are a soup lover. " ~ Amazon Customer

"I love this book! I usually make up 2-3 batches of soup over the weekend and freeze individual portion sizes for my lunch throughout the week. I especially love the beginning of the book where Carrie goes into detail and provides tips on purchasing produce, the type of equipment you'll need, and loads of other interesting information. HIGHLY RECOMMEND!" ~ Jessica

"I am in love with the "KETO Soup Bowl" recipe book! The recipes are easy to follow and incredibly delicious. The recipes made with pureed cauliflower are the best I have ever had. I don't consider myself a great cook by any means and these tasty recipes have me feeling like an all-star chef. Best of all, they are totally healthy. I will forever use these recipes to create delicious soups. BTW, my picky children have enjoyed many of the recipes too (Sausage and Kale, Turkey Pot Pie, Confetti Veggie). HIGHLY RECOMMENDED!" ~ Steph

www.carriebrown.com

SOUP HOW TO

There's not a lot that's critical to making great soup. A good recipe, fresh, quality ingredients, some basic chopping skills and you're good to go, but if you're not used to cooking non-starchy veggies, there's a few things that might help you get fantastic results from the get-go. And I want you to have that joy. So here's a few tips and tricks to enhance those 3 things to best use for making fantastic soups.

Buying veggies

These days, unless you shop at a farmers market, you are often given two options for buying the same vegetable: trimmed (and packaged) or untrimmed. Typically the trimmed, packaged version is more expensive, and historically I've always gone straight for the untrimmed, cheaper option because hey, I can just cut all the leaves and roots off with the best of them. However, when I was standing in Trader Joe's, staring at all the produce, and preparing for a soup-making marathon one weekend to develop recipes for this book, I had a long hard think about whether one option was actually better than the other.

Here's some things to think about:

- Time v. money – depending on what you have more of, or value more right now – time or money – will determine whether it makes sense to spend a little extra getting trimmed veggies that save you time, or spend a little less getting untrimmed veggies that take some work.

- Cost per pound – while it is true that at first glance the untrimmed veggies are cheaper per pound, you are also paying for the parts you discard. If you take that into account, you might find the price per pound of usable produce is about the same as the price per pound of the trimmed and packaged version. What you really need to compare is price per usable pound.

- What you're getting – the trimming process can often reveal flaws that wouldn't make the grade for trimmed and packaged produce. It wouldn't be the first time I've cut into some seemingly healthy veggie to find some badness lurking within. You rarely have that happen with trimmed produce - typically you can use every last bit. The same cannot always be said for untrimmed.

- Speed and ease – there will be occasions when you have all the time in the world to remove the outer leaves, trim the stalk and then lovingly shave a pound of Brussels Sprouts. And other times you just need to get dinner on the table, so being able to pour pre-trimmed, pre-shaved sprouts into the pan is an absolute godsend. Most important, perhaps, is doing what will encourage you to make more soup, and thus eat more veggies. If the thought of having to trim your way through pounds of veggies every week leaves you less likely to put in the effort, buy the trimmed option.

There is no right or wrong. Untrimmed are not a healthier option. Do whatever works best for you – and remember that may change with each trip to the store. For my soup-making marathon you can bet I was all trimmed all the way!

Weighing veggies

I said this earlier, but it is worth repeating. The weight of veggies indicated in the recipe is usable produce – the amount of each vegetable that you can actually use. It does not include all the roots and leaves and trimmings.

Do I recommend that you use the exact weights of veggies as given in the recipe? Yes, you will get a consistently successful soup if you do. Does it really matter if the weight of the veggies is not exact? No, but the flavor will be different and the consistency will be different – how much different depends on how much more or less of the veggie that you use.

Preparing veggies

Now you've got your veggies home and ready to get your soup on, let's talk a little bit about preparing them. This assumes that you either bought trimmed veggies, or that you have trimmed them yourself to discard any roots, leaves and stalks that you don't want.

Before you spend one second with a knife in your hand, read the recipe through, because this could save you a whole bunch of time and effort.

- If it is a completely blended soup then your veggies don't have to be beautiful. Don't spend time on them – just cut them into small, similar sized chunks and call it good. Don't cry over an onion making beautiful dice if it is just going to be blended smooth. Chop, chop, chop and you're done.

- Don't peel the veggies unless the recipe states – you'll be throwing away some precious nutrients if you do. My peeler is one of my least used kitchen utensils. If your veggies are dirty, give them a quick scrub.

Once you've determined what your veggies need to look like, you're ready to get on with the chopping. But why chop at all if you're just going to blend it all into a liquid? There's two main reasons for a little chopping action before you cook your veggies:

- Chopping allows you to spot any bad bits easier so you can remove them.

- Chopping all your veggies into small, similar sized pieces will mean they cook quicker and more evenly. If you're chopping cauliflower or broccoli, cut the florets into quarters through the stem since this is the densest part.

Cooking veggies

Cook the veggies per the instructions in the recipe. Even though most times they are going to be blended, you still don't want to overcook them. Overcooked veggies just don't have the same flavor. Use the tip of a knife to determine when they are tender, or carefully fish a piece out and eat it.

Where a recipe says "crisp tender" it means there's just a little hint of crunch when you bite into it.

Transferring from pan to blender

When the veggies are cooked and you're ready to transfer them to the blender, remember that the contents of the pan are very hot. In my soup-making excitement I have forgotten this basic fact on more than one occasion. Ouch.

I have found that the easiest, safest, and cleanest way to do this – because we do love less clean-up – is to hold the blender jug right next to the pan, and using a ladle, spoon the veggies into the jug. Once the veggies are all removed, place the blender jug on the counter and using both hands, carefully tip the hot liquid from the pan into the blender jug. Don't forget to use oven mitts if you have pans that do not have cool-touch handles. If you try and tip the veggies and liquid into the blender jug at the same time you will splash hot liquid everywhere and you'll be sad. At the very least you'll have a mess to clean up, and you could end up with a burn.

Blending

The most important piece of advice I can give you with regard to blending is a *what not to do*. Don't forget to put the lid on before you start blending. Trust me on this one.

There will be times when you don't want to blend your soup to a smooth puree, but want to keep some texture in it. The Green Bean Casserole Soup is a great example. The recipe instructions will guide you when to whack that knob up to high and when to leave it tinkering down the low end.

When adding guar gum and konjac flour, or at other times when the recipes calls for low speed, always have the blender set accordingly. By low speed I mean that the blender is running just fast enough to create a vortex in the soup but no higher.

Making soup in batches when your blender won't hold it all

Since veggies take up much more space before they are blended, even the biggest blending jugs can struggle to fit all those fabulous veggies into them in one go. The answer to this problem is to blend in batches. Here's how to do that successfully:

1. Using a ladle, carefully spoon some of the veggies and some of the hot liquid into the blender jug.

2. Blend to the smoothness and consistency required in the recipe.

3. Pour ¾ of this batch of blended veggies into a bowl – I use my melamine pouring batter

bowls because the spout and handle make them perfect for this job.

4. Repeat steps 1 – 3 until all the veggies and liquid have been removed from the pan. To the last batch of veggies add the additional ingredients as stated in the recipe.

5. Once the final batch of veggies have been blended to the right consistency along with any additional ingredients, pour the soup in the blender jug and the soup in the bowl back into the pan and stir well to completely combine all the batches together.

6. If serving your soup immediately, warm it gently, if necessary, before eating.

Thickening or thinning your soups

I like a big, steaming bowl of thick, creamy soup. They make me feel way more comforted and satiated than thin, brothy soups. So naturally, that's my go-to when I start many new recipes. If you like your soups thinner or you want them to stretch further, soup-thinning is really easy.

Once your soup is finished, and you've given it a few minutes to completely thicken, if you want it thinner, add ½ cup stock at a time and stir well. Continue to add in ½ cup increments until it is the thickness you and your tribe like.

If you need to thicken your soup, sprinkle ½ tsp. konjac flour over the surface of the soup while whisking rapidly. Leave for several minutes to fully thicken, and then repeat if necessary.

Storing the soup

If you are making soup to store or to freeze, make sure that it is completely cool before sealing your storage container. If you seal the container while the soup is still warm, condensation will dilute your soup and make it watery. I am pretty sure you don't want watery soup.

I store my soup in Pyrex 7-cup round glass storage containers. I ladle the soup from the pan to the container and then leave the soup to cool without putting the lid on until it is cold.

Freezing, defrosting, and reheating the soup

All the blended soups freeze very well. I would exercise caution when freezing unblended soups – soups that have large pieces of vegetables in them, as you may find that the vegetables become soggy once defrosted, just like some frozen vegetables do.

To defrost, leave your soups out overnight. If your soup has separated, re-blend or use an immersion blender to get its smooth consistency back. A quick blend and all will be well.

When re-heating your soups – either in a pan or a microwave – do so gently & just until warmed through, otherwise you will overcook the veggies and end up with a mushy consistency and taste. Just because they are already liquidized doesn't mean you can't push them past their best.

www.carriebrown.com

SERVING SIZES AND MACRO CALCULATIONS

Serving Sizes

You will notice that there are no serving sizes noted on the recipes. That's because a serving size is however much you eat. It's not helpful to have some stranger tell you the amount of food to eat when they know nothing about you. I can't help you to know when you have reached satiety, how much or what you've already eaten that day, how much more you need to eat and of what (if you are tracking to specific macros), what your goals are, how much you weigh, how physically active you are, where you are on your journey, or anything else that would determine an appropriate amount for you to consume. With KETO the focus is very much on eating to your unique needs.

The recipes all produce about 2 quarts / 4 pints / 8 cups of soup, which will typically serve 4 – 6 people, depending on whether it was being eaten as a starter, a main dish, or a side dish. Most of the recipes can be extended by following the thinning instructions on page 20.

Macro Calculations

We do not provide macro calculations for these recipes. Here's why: if we did they would be mostly inaccurate compared to what you actually ate, and we are not in the business of giving you erroneous or potentially harmful information. Calculating macros for recipes is highly inaccurate, because of the sheer number of variables in ingredients available. When we tested several online calculators, the exact same recipes all gave us different answers. How helpful is that?! Which answers were right? No one knows. Add to that, if you don't use exactly the same amounts of exactly the same ingredients we used then our data will be even more inaccurate.

If you do choose to track macros, the only way to get figures that are somewhat accurate is to punch the exact amounts of the exact ingredients you used in to an reliable online calculator, and then divide it by the amount you actually ate. Even then, please understand the limitations of the online tools versus the enormous variables in play. We strongly recommend you DO NOT use My Fitness Pal or any other calculator that is driven by consumer entered data.

There are way too many variables for us give you accurate macro data, so we decided in your best interests to leave that in your own very capable hands.

~~~~~~

If you do find you still have questions about ingredients, equipment, or recipes – after checking out the online info at the links included on page 5 – there's a Q&A page for this cookbook on my website. Head there and see if the answer is already waiting for you. Feel free to add new questions in the comments and I will update the page with answers as they come in.

THE KETO SOUP BOWL Q&A

www.carriebrown.com/keto-soup-bowl-cookbook-qa

Bacon and Brussels Sprouts Chowder

Prep: 10 mins | Cook: 20 mins | Total: 30 mins

12 oz. / 340g bacon

2 ½ cups / 1 ¼ pints chicken stock

1 lb. / 450g cauliflower, roughly chopped

¼ cup / 2 fl oz. heavy cream **SUB: thick coconut milk for dairy-free**

½ tsp. sea salt

1 lb. / 450g shredded Brussels Sprouts

½ tsp. konjac flour (glucomannan power)

½ tsp. guar gum

Cook the bacon to your preferred degree of doneness. For me that means laying the strips (rashers) on a baking tray – one with sides unless you want to spend the afternoon cleaning your oven – and popping in the center of the oven at 400ºF for 15 minutes. Leave to cool and then cut into pieces using a pair of kitchen scissors. It's just easier with scissors. Try not to eat any bacon pieces. Even one piece puts you at risk of eating the whole lot. Don't ask me how I know this.

In a large pan or stock pot, put the stock and cauliflower, bring to the boil, cover, and simmer for about 15 minutes until the cauliflower is very soft.

Transfer the stock and cauliflower to the blender, add the cream and sea salt, and blend on high until very smooth. Very.

Meanwhile, place the shredded Brussels in the pan with a cup of water, bring to the boil and simmer until crisp-tender, about 10 minutes. When done, drain very well.

Back over at the blender, turn the speed to low, and slowly tap the konjac flour, then the guar gum through the opening in the lid. Blend for 5 seconds.

Pour the soup back into the pan, and add the bacon pieces and drained Brussels. Stir well and warm gently if necessary.

~~~~~~

If you think you don't like Brussels Sprouts, this chowder will change your mind by the second spoonful. I have converted an army of Brussels Sprouts Haters to Brussels Sprouts Lovers with this recipe.

PS. Dear Brits, I don't know why Americans put an 's' on the end of Brussel either, but they do, and since there are more of them to call me out in a typo, I went with it. Forgive me?

www.carriebrown.com

Lasagna Soup

Prep: 10 mins | Cook: 20 mins | Total: 30 mins

1 lb. / 450g ground (minced) beef

2 cups / 1 pint beef stock

1 lb. / 450g cauliflower, roughly chopped

1 tsp. dried oregano

½ cup / 4 fl oz. thick coconut milk

½ tsp. sea salt

Ground black pepper to taste

½ tsp. konjac flour (glucomannan power)

½ tsp. guar gum

6 oz. / 170g sharp (strong) Cheddar cheese, grated **OMIT for dairy-free**

1 lb. 8 oz. / 670g canned plum tomatoes, drained well and chopped

Cook the beef in a large pan or stock pot over a low heat until browned, breaking it up into small pieces as it cooks.

Meanwhile, in another pan, put the stock, oregano, and cauliflower, bring to the boil, cover, and simmer for about 15 minutes until the cauliflower is very soft.

Transfer the stock and cauliflower to the blender, add the thick coconut milk, sea salt, and pepper, and blend on high until very smooth.

Turn the blender to low, and slowly tap the konjac flour, then the guar gum through the opening in the lid. Blend for 5 seconds.

Pour the soup into the pan with the browned beef, and add the grated cheese and drained, chopped tomatoes. Stir well and warm gently if necessary.

~~~~~~

Shut your eyes and eat a spoonful: it tastes exactly like a mouthful of lasagna. The only difference is it comes in a bowl, has no pasta to make you fat and unhappy, is three-quarters vegetables and takes just 30 minutes to make instead of hours. Not to mention it is oh so easy to transport and reheat for lunch the next day. I even ate it for breakfast. This stuff is the bomb.

Top tip: Vary the fat:protein ratio by using different leanness of ground beef. Anything from 90/10 to 70/30. Adjust to your taste, budget, availability, macro, health, and fat-loss goals.

Top tip: Sub heavy cream for the thick coconut milk if you prefer, or have it on hand.

www.carriebrown.com

Salmon and Leek Chowder

Prep: 10 mins | Cook: 35 mins | Total: 45 mins

1½ lb. / 670g salmon fillets

2 cups / 1 pint chicken stock

14 oz. / 390g celery, roughly chopped

11 oz. / 310g zucchini (courgettes), peeled and roughly chopped

1 tsp. dried dill

¼ cup / 2 fl oz. heavy cream **SUB: thick coconut milk for dairy-free**

½ tsp. sea salt

Ground black pepper to taste

2 TBSP coconut oil or avocado oil

1 lb. / 450g leeks, finely sliced

½ tsp. konjac flour (glucomannan power)

½ tsp. guar gum

Poach the salmon with the chicken stock in a large pan or stock pot over a medium heat until the salmon just starts to flake apart. Using a slotted spoon, remove the salmon and reserve.

Add the celery, zucchini (courgettes), and dill to the pot with the stock and fish juices and bring to the boil. Reduce heat, cover and simmer for about 10 minutes until the vegetables are soft.

Transfer the stock and veggies to the blender, add the cream, sea salt, pepper, and dill, and blend on high until very smooth.

Meanwhile, melt the coconut or avocado oil in the pan, add the finely sliced leeks, cover and sauté over low heat for 15 minutes until the leeks are soft.

Turn the blender to low, and slowly tap the konjac flour, then the guar gum through the opening in the lid. Blend for 5 seconds.

Pour the soup into the pan with the sautéed leeks and stir well.

Flake the salmon fillets and add the pieces to the pan with the leeks and soup. Gently stir to mix through and warm gently if necessary.

~~~~~~

Holy mother of yumness, Batman.

Top tip: Sub thick coconut milk for the heavy cream for dairy-free, or if you just have it on hand.

www.carriebrown.com

Chicken and Mushroom Soup Uncanned

Prep: 10 mins | Cook: 20 mins | Total: 30 mins

2 cups / 1 pint chicken stock

1 lb. / 450g celery, roughly chopped

8 oz. / 225g cauliflower, roughly chopped

2 TBSP coconut oil or avocado oil

1 lb. / 450g chicken, cut into small pieces

8 oz. / 225g mushrooms, cut into small pieces

¼ cup / 2 fl oz. heavy cream **SUB: thick coconut milk for dairy-free**

½ tsp. sea salt

1 TBSP finely chopped fresh sage

1 tsp. konjac flour (glucomannan power)

½ tsp. guar gum

Put the stock, celery, and cauliflower in a pan, bring to the boil, cover, and simmer for about 15 minutes until the veggies are very soft.

Meanwhile, in a large pan sauté the chicken pieces in the coconut or avocado oil for 10 minutes. Add the chopped mushrooms and sauté for another 5 minutes. Remove from the heat and set aside.

Transfer the stock, celery, and cauliflower to the blender, add the cream, sea salt, and sage, and blend on high until very smooth. It will be super thick. Stay with me on this one.

Turn the blender to low, and slowly tap the konjac flour, then the guar gum through the opening in the lid. Blend for 5 seconds.

Pour the soup into the pan with the sautéed chicken, mushrooms, and juices and stir well. Warm gently if necessary.

~~~~~~

In the spirit of full disclosure, this tastes absolutely nothing like Campbell's Cream of Chicken and Mushroom Soup. NOTHING. It does, however, taste like freshly sautéed chicken and mushroom pieces in a delicious, thick and creamy soup base.

I don't mean to disappoint you, but there are no natural ingredients on this earth that can recreate the taste of the chemical soup that comes forth from many a grocery store can (tin). Instead of chemicals, there's 2 lbs. of fresh veggies and 1 lb. fresh chicken in this sucker. Take that, "soup" manufacturers!

Sausage and Kale Soup

Prep: 10 mins | Cook: 15 mins | Total: 25 mins

3 cups / 1 ½ pints chicken stock

12 oz. / 335g tomatoes, roughly chopped

8 oz. / 225g celery, roughly chopped

1 tsp. dried basil

1 tsp. sea salt

½ tsp. konjac flour (glucomannan powder)

6 oz. / 170g kale, shredded and the stems removed

12 oz. / 335g pre-cooked sausages, cut in half lengthwise and then sliced

Put the stock, tomatoes, and celery in a pan, bring to the boil, cover, and simmer for 5 minutes.

Transfer the stock and veggies to the blender, add the basil and sea salt, and blend on high until very smooth.

Turn the blender to low, and slowly tap the konjac flour through the opening in the lid. Blend for 5 seconds.

Pour the soup back into the pan and bring to the boil.

Reduce the heat until it is simmering, add the kale and the sausage, and simmer for 10 minutes until the kale is completely wilted.

~~~~~~

I am not a lover of kale, but given my goal of creating 50 new soup recipes composed of a variety veggies, it was hard to keep walking right on past the striking dark green leaves stacked so lovingly in the produce department of my local Trader Joe's without depositing some in my cart (trolley). I kept reminding myself that while I may not enjoy kale's vitamin-laden charms, there are plenty of people who do.

I got the idea for pairing it with sausages from a podcast that I recorded where we talked about kale. "Don't try to eat it raw!" the other host exclaimed. "Get the kale to cook down with some nice, healthy, tasty fats! Cook it with sausages!"

The next thing I knew I was making an on-air commitment to millions of listeners that I would create some deliciousness with kale and sausages. So this one's for all you kale lovers out there, and all you kale haters, too. Because this might just be the recipe that has you eating kale like it was your favorite food.

www.carriebrown.com

Prawn Cocktail Gazpacho

Prep: 10 mins | Cook: 5 mins | Total: 15 mins

1 cup / 8 fl oz. chicken stock

1 lb. 2 oz. / 500g fresh tomatoes, roughly chopped

4 oz. / 110g celery, roughly chopped

½ tsp. fresh rosemary, finely chopped

1 tsp. sea salt

Ground black pepper to taste

½ cup / 4 fl oz. full-fat Greek yogurt (DO NOT USE FAT-FREE it will separate when heated!)

½ tsp. konjac flour (glucomannan power)

1 tsp. guar gum

1 lb. / 450g prawns or shrimp, pre-cooked and peeled

Put the stock, tomatoes, celery, rosemary, sea salt, pepper, and yogurt in the blender and blend on high speed until very smooth. This will take some time since the veggies are not cooked first. Don't give up!

Once smooth, turn the blender to low, and slowly tap the konjac flour, then the guar gum through the opening in the lid. Blend for 5 seconds.

Roughly chop the prawns into smaller pieces and add to the soup.

~~~~~~

Need grub in a hurry? Shove some stuff in a blender, whizz it up, and add prawns. Dinner = done.

Top Tip: Thaw frozen prawns in a heartbeat by placing them in a sieve or colander and running warm water over them for a minute or two. Drain well, shake to remove any excess water, and then spread on kitchen paper and pat dry.

Top Tip: Stock up on frozen prawns whenever they are on sale. Pre-cooked, peeled prawns thaw in a couple of minutes and sauté or warm through in another two, providing some fantastic protein in the blink of an eye. I always have some in the freezer for when I need a meal real fast.

While a gazpacho is intended to be raw vegetables, this is also lovely heated up if it's cold and something warm is going to hit the spot better.

You can also leave the veggies somewhat chunky if you prefer. Just stop blending before they get smooth.

Thai Chicken Coconut Soup

Prep: 10 mins | Cook: 25 mins | Total: 35 mins

4 cups / 2 pints water

1 ½ inch piece fresh ginger, peeled and finely sliced

1 oz. / 30g fresh cilantro leaves and stalks

1 large lime, zest peeled into wide strips

2 stems lemongrass, halved lengthwise and cut into short pieces

3 TBSP Thai fish sauce

Juice from the lime

3 cups / 1 ½ pints thick coconut milk (2 cans)

1 lb. / 450g chicken, cut into strips

½ large or 1 small red pepper, cut into thin sticks

8 oz. / 225g mushrooms, quartered

Small handful of fresh cilantro leaves

Put the water in a large stock pot with the ginger, cilantro, lime peel, and lemongrass, and bring to the boil.

Add the fish sauce and lime juice, reduce the heat and simmer for 10 minutes.

Strain the broth through a sieve to remove all the flavorings and return the broth to the stock pot. Discard the flavorings.

Add the coconut milk to the broth and bring to the boil. Allow to boil for 2 minutes.

Add the chicken pieces, reduce the heat and simmer for 5 minutes.

Add the mushrooms and the red pepper and simmer for another 5 minutes.

Stir in the fresh cilantro leaves and stir.

~~~~~~

I thought with all the new-to-me ingredients that this soup would be a long, complicated, and drawn-out affair. EASIEST. SOUP. EVER. If I could have only one soup for the rest of my life, this would be it. I adapted it from traditional Tom Ka Gai so it was easier to make, and added red pepper and extra mushrooms to and some extra color and nutrition, but the base tastes just like the real thing. This soup made me grin from ear to ear the moment I took the first taste.

Clam Chowder

Prep: 10 mins | Cook: 20 mins | Total: 30 mins

4 small cans / 26 oz. / 730g chopped clams and juice, drained and juice reserved

Approx. 1 cup / 8 fl oz. chicken stock (see instructions)

1 lb. / 450g cauliflower, roughly chopped

5 oz. / 140g bacon, cut into small pieces

8 oz. / 225g celery, sliced

8 oz. / 225g onion, chopped

¼ cup / 2 fl oz. heavy cream **SUB: thick coconut milk for dairy-free**

½ tsp. sea salt

Ground black pepper to taste

1 tsp. dried dill

1 tsp. konjac flour (glucomannan power)

1 tsp. guar gum

Put the clam juice and enough chicken stock to make 3 cups of total liquid into a large pan or stock pot with the cauliflower, bring to the boil, cover and cook until cauliflower is soft.

Meanwhile, put the bacon in another pan and sauté over medium heat for 5 minutes. Add the celery and onions, cover, and cook until the veggies are just tender, about 15 minutes.

Once the cauliflower is soft, carefully transfer it with the stock to the blender and blend on high until completely smooth. Add the cream, sea salt, pepper, and dill.

Turn the blender to low, and slowly tap the konjac flour, then the guar gum through the opening in the lid. Blend for 5 seconds.

Pour the soup into the pan with the bacon and veggies, and then add the clams. Stir well and heat through.

~~~~~~

Everything that was frustrating about being a new arrival in the US was forgiven the day I discovered {New England} Clam Chowder. To me, Clam Chowder is the ultimate comfort food. It warms and soothes my soul like nothing else. I was literally jumping for joy around the Ketovangelist Kitchen when I ate my first bowl of this recipe and realized we now have Clam Chowder without all those starchy potatoes and we won't even miss them for one millisecond. This is, without doubt, the tastiest way to eat mollusks…ever.

Turkey Pot Pie Gumbo

Prep: 10 mins | Cook: 30 mins | Total: 40 mins

2 ½ cups / 1 ¼ pints chicken stock

1 lb. / 450g turkey, cut into chunks

5 oz. / 140g celery, sliced

5 oz. / 140g onion, diced

6 oz. / 170g radishes, peeled and cubed

4 oz. / 110g broccoli, cut into small florets

1 lb. / 450g cauliflower, roughly chopped

½ tsp. sea salt

Ground black pepper to taste

2 oz. / 50g butter **SUB: ghee for dairy-free**

½ tsp. konjac flour (glucomannan powder)

½ cup fresh parsley sprigs

Put the stock, turkey, celery, onion, and radishes into a large pan or stock pot and bring to the boil over medium heat. Cover, reduce heat and simmer for 10 minutes. Add broccoli and continue simmering until veggies are just tender, about 5 minutes.

Strain the stock through a sieve or colander into a large bowl, return the stock to the pan, and reserve the meat and veggies.

Add the cauliflower to the stock, bring to the boil. Cover, and simmer until the cauliflower is soft.

Carefully transfer the cauliflower and stock to the blender, add the sea salt, pepper, and butter and blend on high until very smooth.

Turn the blender to low, and slowly tap the konjac flour through the opening in the lid. Blend for 5 seconds. Add the parsley and blend for a few seconds until evenly distributed.

Pour the soup back into the pan, add the reserved meat and veggies and stir well. Heat through and serve.

~~~~~~

If you want to use leftovers from a turkey roast, instead of cooking the turkey with the vegetables, add the chopped cooked turkey at the end and heat through.

You can skip peeling the radishes (super pesky task!) but don't be surprised if your soup is pink.

Wild Chicken and Rice Soup

Prep: 10 mins | Cook: 30 mins | Total: 40 mins

2 TBSP coconut or avocado oil

2 lbs. / 900g skinless, boneless chicken, cut into 1" pieces

8 oz. / 225g cream cheese

1 cup / 8 fl oz. heavy cream

1 cup / 8 fl oz. chicken stock

2 tsp. garlic powder

4 tsp. dried thyme

2 TBSP lemon juice

1 tsp. sea salt

ground black pepper

4 oz. / 110g onion, chopped

4 oz. / 110g celery, chopped

1 ½ tsp. konjac flour / glucomannan powder

2 x 8 oz. / 225g packets shirataki rice, rinsed well in cold water and drained well

4 cups / 2 pints chicken stock

Put the oil in a pan over a medium-high heat, add the chicken pieces and sauté until lightly browned. Remove the chicken from the pan and set aside.

To the pan, add the cream cheese, cream, and 8 fl oz. / 1 cup chicken stock, and stir well over medium heat until the cream cheese is melted. Add the garlic powder, thyme, lemon juice, sea salt and ground black pepper, onion, and celery and mix well.

While stirring rapidly with one hand, sprinkle the konjac flour gently over the surface of the sauce and mix well. Add the chicken pieces back into the pan, bring to the boil, reduce the heat and simmer for 15 minutes.

Add the rinsed, drained shirataki rice and final 2 pints / 4 cups chicken stock. Stir well, bring just to the boil and then remove from the heat and serve.

~~~~~~

Top tip: Soup thicker or thinner than you prefer? Adjust using extra stock or konjac flour after you have added the rice.

Never tried shirataki rice? This'll make you a fan. All the comfort, none of the carbs.

Roasted Pepper and Smoked Sausage Soup

Prep: 10 mins | Cook: 30 mins | Total: 40 mins

Coconut or avocado oil spray

1 ½ lbs. / 670g tomatoes, quartered

6 oz. / 170g (approx. 1 large) red pepper, sliced, with core and seeds removed

3 cups / 1 ½ pints beef stock

½ cup / 4 fl oz. thick coconut milk

1 tsp. sea salt

Ground black pepper to taste

3 tsp. coconut aminos

½ tsp. konjac flour (glucomannan powder)

1 lb. pre-cooked smoked or summer sausage of your choice, sliced

Roast the tomatoes and pepper on an oiled baking tray for 30 minutes at 450ºF.

Working in batches, carefully place the vegetables in a blender with the beef stock, coconut milk, sea salt, pepper and coconut aminos and blend until very smooth.

Turn the blender to low and slowly tap the konjac flour through the opening in the lid. Blend for 5 seconds. Pour all batches of soup back into the stock pot and stir well.

Cut the cooked sausages into bite-sized chunks and add to the soup. Heat the soup until the sausages are warmed through.

~~~~~~

This tomato soup has a wee bit of a spicy kick to it. I say "wee" because my tolerance for spiciness is a big, fat zero. Spicy food lovers everywhere will taste this and go, "What spiciness??" It's definitely not hot, it's just intense tomato with a zing.

The zing comes from the roasting, the red peppers, and the coconut aminos, which we use on KETO instead of Worcestershire Sauce. But let's talk about Worcestershire Sauce for a minute. More specifically, let's talk about pronouncing Worcestershire. It's "Wuss-ter-sheer", not "Wore-sess-ter-shire". I remember the first time I heard a Canadian say Worcestershire. When I figured out what they were referring to, I laughed my socks right off; not to be mean, but because it sounded so long and funny to an English person. For those not familiar with such things, Worcester (Wuss-ter) is a very pretty little town, and Worcestershire (Wuss-ter-sheer) a county, in England. So, the other benefit of using coconut aminos instead of Worcestershire Sauce is that you don't have to have an English lesson on pronunciation. #WINNING.

Sausage, Fennel and Leek Hodgepodge

Prep: 10 mins | Cook: 20 mins | Total: 30mins

1 lb. ground sausage (sausagemeat)

1 lb. / 450g leeks, very thinly sliced

4 cups / 2 pints chicken stock

13 oz. / 365g (approx. 2 bulbs) fennel, roughly chopped

1 tsp. sea salt

2 oz. / 55g butter **SUB: ghee for dairy-free**

½ tsp. konjac flour (glucomannan powder)

Brown the ground sausage in a large pan or stock pot over a medium heat, breaking it up with a spatula as you cook it. Once it is browned, remove it from the pan using a slotted spoon to leave the pork fat behind in the pan, and reserve the meat.

Place the pan with the pork fat over a low heat, add the thinly sliced leeks, and sauté until just soft, but not browned.

Meanwhile, put the stock and fennel in another pan, and bring to the boil. As soon as the fennel and stock have come to the boil, remove from the heat.

Carefully transfer the stock and fennel to the blender, add the sea salt and butter, and blend FOREVER, until it is very smooth and creamy.

Turn the blender to low, and slowly tap the konjac flour through the opening in the lid. Blend for 5 seconds.

Pour the fennel soup over the sautéed leeks in the large pan, add the browned sausage and mix well. Warm gently if required.

~~~~~~

This is one thick and hearty bowl of scrumptious goodness! Not to mention that this is the recipe that got me over my ridiculous belief that all soups needed to be silky-smooth and lump-free. I discovered that it's the lumpy leeks that totally turn this recipe into soup awesomeness.

One of the tricks to success here is not over-cooking the leeks when you are sautéing them – leave them with a tiny bit of crunch so they don't disappear into the fennel soup base. I love how leaving the leeks whole means you get the two separate flavors in the same mouthful.

If you're like me and thought you liked your soup lump-less, give this one a shot and see if you're converted to loving lumpy, bumpy soup.

Chicken Tortilla Soup

Prep time: 10 mins | Cook time: 15 mins | Total time: 25mins

1 cup / 8 fl oz. water

10 oz. / 280g shredded white cabbage

4 cups / 2 pints chicken stock

8 oz. / 225g celery, roughly chopped

8 oz. / 225g cauliflower, roughly chopped

6 oz. / 170g tomato paste

1 tsp. chopped fresh dill

½ tsp. sea salt

Ground black pepper to taste

1 tsp. cumin seeds

2 oz. / 55g butter **SUB: ghee for dairy-free**

½ tsp. konjac flour (glucomannan powder)

1 lb. cooked chicken, shredded

Place the water and cabbage in a pan, covered, over medium heat, and sauté until crisp-tender – about 5 minutes. Don't overcook it – you want the cabbage to have a crunch to it. Drain well in a colander, return cabbage to the dry pan and reserve.

Meanwhile, place the stock, veggies, and tomato paste in a pan, bring to the boil and simmer for about 15 minutes until soft.

Transfer the stock and veggies (not the cabbage!) to a blender and blend on high until very smooth.

Add the dill, sea salt, pepper, cumin, and butter, and blend to mix.

Turn the blender to low, and slowly tap the konjac flour through the opening in the lid. Blend for 5 seconds.

Pour the tomato soup over the cabbage and mix well. Add the cooked, shredded chicken and warm the soup through.

~~~~~~

According to my lovely Roomie, this is the closest thing to Tortilla Soup she's ever tasted. The only thing you'll be missing is a little crunch, and if you ate some pork rinds with it you wouldn't even be missing that. You all asked me for KETO Chicken Tortilla Soup, and baby, you got it!

Chilled Avocado Cream with Prawns

Prep: 10 mins | Cook: 0 mins | Total: 10 mins

1 lb. / 450g avocado flesh (about 3 medium avocados)

2 TBSP lemon juice

2 cups / 1 pint chicken stock

½ cup / 4 fl oz. heavy cream **SUB: thick coconut milk for dairy-free**

1 cup / 8 fl oz. almond milk

1 TBSP coconut aminos

Sea salt and ground black pepper to taste

1 lb. / 450g cooked, peeled prawns

2 large tomatoes, chopped into small dice

Fresh basil leaves

½ cup / 4 fl oz. sour cream **SUB: thick coconut milk for dairy-free**

Peel the avocados, remove the pit, and chop them into rough chunks. Place the avocado in a blender with the lemon juice and blend well. You may need to stop, scrape, and start a few times as avocado is very thick.

Add the chicken stock, cream, almond milk, coconut aminos, sea salt and ground black pepper and blend until completely smooth.

Chill.

When ready to serve, remove from the 'fridge, pour into serving bowls and add the prawns and tomatoes to the top of the soup.

Garnish with a large dollop of sour cream and fresh chopped basil.

~~~~~~

Over in our Ketovangelist Kitchen Facebook Group, we sometimes get folks who pop in and ask how they can eat avocado – either because they don't like the texture of fresh avocado, they don't care for the taste of plain avocado, or they're just bored of eating naked avocado.

So this delicious, crazy-fast, healthy-fat crammed bowl of goodness is for all the avocado lovers AND all the I-want-to-love-avocado-more peeps.

This is also a great way to use up the avocados that you know are going to be past their best by tomorrow. Got avocados? Soup 'em!

Chicken Noodle Soup

Prep: 15 mins | Cook: 20 mins | Total: 35 mins

2 TBSP coconut or avocado oil

2 oz. / 55 g butter **SUB: ghee for dairy-free**

3 oz. / 85g onion, finely chopped

3 cloves garlic, finely chopped

6 oz. / 170g celery, finely chopped

Sea salt and ground black pepper to taste

1 tsp. dried thyme

1 lb. / 450g chicken, cut into small pieces

3 cups / 1 ½ pints chicken stock (homemade is best, but otherwise from the store)

½ tsp. konjac flour (glucomannan power) *optional

8 oz. / 225 g Miracle Noodles Fettucine, rinsed very well in water, and then drained

Melt the coconut or avocado oil and butter over medium heat in a large pan. Add the onion, garlic, celery, sea salt, black pepper, and dried thyme, and sauté until the onion is transparent, about 10 minutes.

Add the chicken pieces and continue to sauté for 5 minutes.

Add the chicken stock, stir well, and bring to the boil.

Lower the heat and simmer for 5 minutes.

If you want a little more body to your soup, sprinkle the konjac flour gently and evenly over the surface of the soup while whisking rapidly. This won't make it thick, it will just make it not stock-thin. It also helps stop the oil and butter making a film on the surface of the soup.

Cut the Miracle Noodles into shorter lengths and stir them into the soup.

Continue heating the soup until the noodles are heated through, then serve.

~~~~~~

The taste testers were wildly enthusiastic about this KETO Chicken Noodle Soup.

"Not only is this really delicious, but my super-picky kids just gobbled it up – Miracle Noodles and all. Didn't even notice they weren't 'normal' wheat noodles. We all absolutely loved it!" - Alisen

Bacon BBQ Chicken Soup

Prep: 10 mins | Cook: 20 mins | Total: 30 mins

12 oz. / 335g bacon, chopped

5 oz. / 140g onion, chopped

10 oz. / 280 g riced cauliflower

1 cup / 8 fl oz. crushed tomatoes (unsweetened, canned)

4 TBSP apple cider vinegar

2 tsp. liquid smoke

3 cups / 1 ½ pints chicken stock

4 tsp. maple extract

½ tsp. guar gum

1 lb. / 450 g chopped, cooked chicken

sea salt and ground black pepper to taste

Put the chopped bacon and onion in a large pan over medium heat and sauté until lightly browned, about 10 minutes.

Add the riced cauliflower, tomatoes, apple cider vinegar, liquid smoke, stock, and maple extract, and stir well.

Bring to the boil and then reduce the heat and simmer for 10 minutes. Carefully transfer the soup to a blender and blend until very smooth.

Turn the blender to low and slowly tap the guar gum through the opening in the lid. Blend for 5 seconds and then pour the soup back into the pan.

Add the cooked chicken pieces and season to taste. Heat until chicken is warmed through and serve.

~~~~~~

This is a riff on a BBQ Sauce that I made for my partner in podcast crime, Brian Williamson, when he and his lovely wife came to visit me in Seattle. That Sauce was wildly successful and it's become the recipe that just keeps on giving. It inspired the Bacon Ripple for the Maple Bacon Crack Ice Cream in my cookbook, The KETO Ice Cream Scoop, and then it inspired this fantastically tasty soup.

Top Tip: if you want this soup to be thinner – DO NOT leave out the guar gum, but add another 1 cup / 8 fl oz. stock. The guar gum is not there to thicken, but to emulsify, and you need it for best results. Make the soup as directed and then stir in an extra cup of stock at the end.

Beef Barlesque Stew

Prep: 10 mins | Cook: 50 mins | Total: 60 mins

2 TBSP coconut or avocado oil

2 lbs. / 900g beef, cubed (I used tri-tip but use the cut that fits your goals and budget)

6 oz. / 170g onion, finely chopped

6 cloves garlic, finely chopped

6 oz. / 170g celery, finely chopped

4 cups / 2 pints pint beef stock

4 oz. / 110g celeriac (celery root), grated

1 beef stock / bouillon cube

8 oz. / 225g Miracle Rice, rinsed very well in water, and then drained

sea salt and ground black pepper

½ tsp. konjac flour (glucomannan power)

Melt the coconut or avocado oil over medium heat in a large pan. Add the cubed beef and brown on all sides. Remove the beef from the pan and reserve.

Add the onion, garlic, and celery to the pan and sauté until the onion is transparent, about 10 minutes.

Add the browned beef back to the pan and add the stock and grated celeriac. Stir well. Bring to the boil, then reduce the heat and simmer for 20 minutes.

Add the well rinsed and drained Miracle Rice and stir well. Continue to simmer for a further 10 minutes. Season with sea salt and ground black pepper to taste.

Sprinkle the konjac flour gently and evenly over the surface of the soup while whisking rapidly. Continue to heat for an additional 2 minutes, then remove from the heat and serve.

~~~~~~

"We want Beef Barley Soup!" was one of the resounding responses that I received when I asked Facebook what soups you miss most now that you're living a KETO lifestyle.

So here, for your tasting pleasure is a hearty beef soup using Miracle Rice where the barley used to be. And while it doesn't have the nutty taste of barley, you'll totally forget there's no grains in this.

To dial your fat up or down, alter the cut of beef you use. Tri-tip is a super-fatty cut of beef, so is very tender and tasty, but you could use brisket or stewing beef instead.

The MadLove Burger Bowl

Prep: 10 mins | Cook: 25 mins | Total: 35 mins

1 lb. / 450g ground (minced) beef

8 oz. / 225g cauliflower, roughly chopped

3 cup / 1½ pints beef stock

½ cup / 4 fl oz. heavy cream **SUB: thick coconut milk for dairy-free**

sea salt and ground black pepper

½ tsp. konjac flour (glucomannan power)

3 oz. / 85g strong cheddar cheese, grated **OMIT for dairy-free**

5 oz. / 140g fresh tomatoes, finely chopped

8 oz. / 225g bacon, cooked and chopped

2 oz. / 55g onion, finely chopped

1 oz. / 30g dill pickle, finely chopped

1 large avocado, peeled, pitted, and chopped

Add the ground beef to a pan over medium heat and sauté until the meat is browned, breaking it up as it cooks. Once browned, remove the beef with a slotted spoon and reserve.

Add the cauliflower and stock to the pan over a medium heat and simmer for 15 minutes.

Carefully transfer the cauliflower and stock to a blender and blend on high until completely smooth. Add the cream, season to taste with sea salt and ground black pepper, and blend until combined.

Turn the blender to low, and slowly tap the konjac flour through the opening in the lid. Blend for 5 seconds.

Pour the blended stock mixture back into the pan and add the beef and grated cheese. Stir until the cheese is completely melted.

And the tomatoes, bacon, onion, and pickle and stir through. Heat the soup just until it is warmed through.

Ladle into serving bowls and top with avocado and cheese chips. Add some extra bacon and tomato as toppings if you want. For the full effect, serve with crisp Romaine lettuce.

~~~~~~

In honor of my favorite Red Robin Burger: The MadLove Burger I give it to you in a bowl that you can whip up and eat at home. You're welcome.

www.carriebrown.com

The Ham's In A Pickle Hodgepodge

Prep: 10 mins | Cook: 30 mins | Total: 40 mins

2 TBSP coconut or avocado oil

4 oz. / 110g onion, finely chopped

3 cloves garlic, finely chopped

7 oz. / 195 g dill pickles, finely chopped

10 oz. / 280g celeriac (celery root), peeled and finely diced

1 lb. / 450g ham, finely cubed (I used smoked ham which gives it a deeper flavor)

3 cups / 1 ½ pints chicken stock

½ cup / 4 fl oz. pickle juice (drained from the jar of dill pickles)

1 TBSP coconut aminos

1 tsp. dried dill

7 oz. / 195g crème fraiche (sub with sour cream if you can't find crème fraiche) **SUB: thick coconut milk for dairy-free**

sea salt and ground black pepper to taste

1 tsp. konjac flour (glucomannan power)

Melt the coconut or avocado oil over medium heat in a large pan or stock pot. Add the onion and garlic and sauté until the onion is lightly browned, about 10 minutes.

Add the chopped dill pickles, celeriac, ham, stock, pickle juice, coconut aminos, and dried dill and stir well. Bring to the boil, reduce the heat and simmer for 15 minutes until the celeriac is tender.

Reduce the heat to low, add the crème fraiche and stir well. Season to taste with sea salt and ground black pepper. NOTE: Some pickles are salty enough without the addition of sea salt.

Gently sprinkle the konjac flour over the surface of the soup while whisking rapidly. Leave to thicken for a couple of minutes, then spoon into bowls and serve.

~~~~~~

If you've been around KETO for a while you'll know that dill pickles are a big deal. Many folks eat them and / or drink pickle juice because they find they really combat the cravings, as well as help with getting the electrolyte balance right.

But as a girl who spent 4 years of her teenage weekends and holidays up to her arms in freezing cold pickles in a McDonald's walk-in fridge, pickles ain't anywhere on my menu. So when the crowds started roaring for Pickle Soup, the prospect was not an appealing one. I am thrilled to report that this soup changed my mind on the whole pickle topic. Because DELISH!

Smoky Hazelnut Turkey Soup

Prep: 10 mins | Cook: 20 mins | Total: 30 mins

2 TBSP butter

5 oz. / 140g onion, finely chopped

1 tsp. smoked paprika

1 lb. / 450g turkey, roughly chopped

4 cup / 2 pints chicken or turkey stock

1 tsp. konjac flour (glucomannan power)

sea salt and ground black pepper to taste

½ cup / 4 fl oz. heavy cream **SUB: thick coconut milk for dairy-free**

3 oz. / 85g toasted hazelnuts, finely chopped

Melt the butter over medium heat in a pan. Add the onion and smoked paprika and sauté until the onion is soft, about 10 minutes.

Add the turkey and stock, and bring just to the boil, then reduce heat and simmer for 5 minutes. If you overcook at this point your turkey will be tough. And no one likes tough turkey.

Carefully transfer the hot soup into a blender and blend on high until it is as smooth as you can get it. It does not get completely smooth, even in a Vitamix. Turn the blender to low, and slowly tap the konjac flour through the opening in the lid. Blend for 5 seconds.

Pour the blended soup back into the pan. Season to taste with sea salt and ground black pepper.

Add the cream and finely chopped hazelnuts and stir well. Heat until warmed through, if necessary.

~~~~~~

Top Tip: if you have leftover turkey meat you can use that instead. In that case, skip the simmering part and add the stock and turkey directly into the blender with the sautéed onions. Then continue as described. Once the soup is finished, heat until warmed through before serving.

This was adapted from a recipe I came across in one of the aged cookbooks I have dragged round the globe with me since I was in my early twenties. At first blush it was rather ordinary tasting. But then I added the cream and toasted hazelnuts and suddenly there were fireworks exploding in my mouth. Those two things totally transform this soup from 'eh' to 'YAY!'

It's probably a very different kind of soup than you've had before. Push those taste bud boundaries! It's also a fantastic new way to use up cooked turkey. Think post-Thanksgiving YUM.

www.carriebrown.com

Drunken Duck Gumbo

Prep: 10 mins | Cook: 20 mins | Total: 30 mins

2 TBSP coconut or avocado oil (or duck fat if you roasted a duck for this)

10 oz. / 280g shredded cabbage

2 TBSP cumin

2 cups / 1 pint chicken stock

2 TBSP white wine

6 oz. / 170g mushrooms, chopped (cremini and / or wild mushrooms are especially good)

½ cup heavy cream **SUB: thick coconut milk for dairy-free**

sea salt to taste

1 tsp. konjac flour (glucomannan power)

1 lb. / 450g cooked duck meat, chopped

Melt the coconut oil, avocado oil, or duck fat over medium heat in a large pan. Add the shredded cabbage and cumin, and sauté until the cabbage is soft, about 15 minutes.

Add the stock and wine and bring just to the boil. Reduce the heat to a simmer and add the chopped mushrooms and cream. Add sea salt to taste and stir well.

Simmer the gumbo for just 5 minutes – you don't want to cook the mushrooms into mush.

Gently sprinkle the konjac flour over the surface of the soup while whisking rapidly. Leave to thicken for a couple of minutes, then add the cooked duck meat, stir and serve.

~~~~~~

I love duck. It is also a very fatty meat – so perfect for KETO. They do tend to be on the pricey side in the US, so more power to you if you or your friends like to go out shooting and manage to snag yourself some in the wild. New to duck? DO IT!!!

I roasted a whole duck in the oven to get my duck meat, but you can also buy duck breasts or legs and use those. You can buy smoked duck if you don't want to cook it at all. And, finally, you can buy ground duck and brown that in a pan to use – although the texture will be different.

The advantages of roasting a whole duck though, are a huge amount of rendered duck fat to use for all your sautéing needs for weeks afterwards, a whole duck carcass to make into an amazing stock, and a house that smells divine for at least a day afterwards. Roasting duck = all goodness.

Top Tip: Even if you are not a wine drinker, I highly recommend that you don't skip it in this recipe. The wine transports this from Duck Soup to Holy Moly Mother of all Soup Deliciousness Drunken Duck Gumbo. You can buy small bottles of white cooking wine if you're not a drinker.

Baconated French Onion Soup

Prep: 10 mins | Cook: 2 hours | Total: 2 hours, 10 mins

12 oz./ 335g bacon, chopped

3 oz. / 85g butter **SUB: ghee for dairy-free**

2 lbs. / 900g onion, thinly sliced

1 lb. / 450g shredded cabbage

½ cup / 4 fl oz. Marsala cooking wine

1 ½ tsp. onion powder

4 ½ cups / 2 pints, 4 fl oz. beef stock

3 TBSP coconut aminos

3 cloves garlic, finely chopped

1 tsp. konjac flour (glucomannan power)

KETO muffins or slices of KETO bread or Cheesy Biscuits (see page 103)

6 oz. / 170g smoked Gruyere cheese **OMIT for dairy-free**

Preheat your oven to 400ºF. Sauté the bacon over medium heat in a large ovenproof pan for 5 minutes. Add the butter, thinly sliced onion and shredded cabbage and stir well to coat the veggies in all the fat. Then sauté for 20 minutes, stirring often.

Stir the veggies and transfer the pan to the oven. Cover the pot, leaving a little gap to allow the veggies to brown better. Cook for an hour, stirring well at the 30-minute mark.

After an hour in the oven, return the pan to the cooktop over a medium heat. Add the Marsala and cook for 5 minutes, scraping all the glorious brown bits off the bottom and sides of the pan.

Add the onion powder, beef stock, coconut aminos, and finely chopped garlic and bring to the boil. Reduce the heat to low and simmer, covered, for 30 minutes.

Gently sprinkle the konjac flour over the surface of the soup while whisking rapidly. Leave to thicken for a couple of minutes, then spoon into serving bowls.

Drop your KETO muffins or KETO bread of choice, or your Cheesy Biscuits on top of the soup, and then grate or slice the smoked Gruyere over the top. Place the soup bowls under a broiler (grill) and broil (grill) until the cheese is golden and bubbling.

~~~~~~

Top Tip: To reduce the carb load, use white or yellow onions, not red or sweet onions.

You can use any cheese you like, but the smoked gruyere really adds another layer of depth here.

Loaded Baked Notato Soup

Prep: 15 mins | Cook: 15 mins | Total: 30 mins

8 oz. / 225g celeriac / celery root, roughly chopped

1 lb. / 450g cauliflower florets, roughly chopped

3 cups / 1 ½ pints chicken stock

¾ cup / 6 fl oz. heavy cream **SUB: thick coconut milk for dairy-free**

2 oz. / 55g butter **SUB: ghee for dairy-free**

1 tsp. nutritional yeast

sea salt and ground black pepper to taste

3 oz. / 85 g strong / sharp Cheddar cheese **OMIT for dairy-free**

¼ cup / 2 fl oz. sour cream **OMIT for dairy-free**

12 oz. / 335g bacon, cooked and chopped

5 green onions / scallions / spring onions, finely sliced

Put the celeriac, cauliflower and stock in a pan over medium heat. Bring to the boil, then reduce the heat and simmer for 15 mins until veggies are very soft.

Carefully transfer the veggies and stock to a blender, add the cream, butter, and nutritional yeast and blend on high until very smooth. Add sea salt and ground black pepper to taste.

Pour the blended soup back into the pan over a low heat and stir in the cheese, sour cream, bacon and onions. Stir until the cheese is completely melted.

Spoon into bowls and garnish with extra grated cheese, bacon pieces, and green onions.

~~~~~~

You were missing your Loaded Baked Potato Soup, weren't you? Well miss it no more!

This is a bowl of thick, glorious comfort that will transport your taste buds back to days of yore without any of that carbage. The taste testers were very confused when they tried it because they knew it couldn't be potato soup because I don't eat potatoes…and yet it tasted totally like potato soup. The beauty of having great KETO recipes: you don't have to give up all your favorite dishes.

Do you need the nutritional yeast? (I know some of you will ask.) No, you don't *need* it, but it tastes better with it. Nutritional yeast is a great thing to have in your KETO pantry and I use it quite a lot. Good news: If you're in the US, Trader Joe's now have it and it is 1/3 the price of the Bragg's, so it's no longer a high-ticket item. Go grab some today!

Chicken and Dumpling Stew

Prep: 15 mins | Cook: 45 mins | Total: 60 mins

2 TBSP coconut or avocado oil

4 oz. / 110g onion, finely chopped

4 oz. / 110g celery, finely chopped

1 batch KETO dumplings (Recipe: www.ketovangelistkitchen.com/dumplings-for-soups-and-stews OR go to www.ketovangelistkitchen.com and search for dumplings)

4 ½ cups / 2 ¼ pints chicken stock

1 chicken stock cube

1 lb. / 450g chicken, cut into small pieces

1 tsp. sea salt

8 oz. / 225g mushrooms, sliced

½ cup / 4 fl oz. heavy cream **SUB: thick coconut milk for dairy-free**

1 TBSP fresh tarragon, finely chopped

Melt the coconut or avocado oil over medium heat in a large pan. Add the onion and celery and sauté until the veggies are just starting to brown, about 15 minutes.

Make the dumpling dough (Recipe: www.ketovangelistkitchen.com/dumplings-for-soups-and-stews OR go to www.ketovangelistkitchen.com and search for dumplings) and leave to rest for 15 minutes.

While the dough is resting, add the chicken stock, stock cube, chicken pieces and sea salt to the veggies in the pan and stir well. Bring the pan to a boil, reduce heat and simmer for 10 minutes.

Roll the dumpling dough per the recipe.

Add the mushrooms to the simmering stew and increase the heat just until it reaches a rolling boil. Carefully spoon the 12 dumplings into the boiling liquid, cover with a lid, and put a timer on for 15 minutes.

Once the timer goes off, lift the lid, gently stir in the cream and fresh chopped tarragon and serve.

~~~~~~

Top Tip: I *highly* recommend reading the recipe for the stew and the dumplings through a few times so that you have a good sense of the order. The most important thing to know is that the dumplings cook less and less fluffy the longer you leave the dough after the 15 minutes of resting time. So, get yourself organized and have the dumplings rested, rolled and ready to drop in the boiling liquid no more than 20 minutes after you make the dough. Mmmmm, dumplings!

All That Mac & Cheese Soup

Prep: 10 mins | Cook: 20 mins | Total: 30 mins

1 lb. / 450g cauliflower, chopped into bite-sized pieces

2 cups / 1 pint almond milk, unsweetened

2 cups / 1 pint chicken stock

4 oz. / 110g cream cheese

¼ cup / 2 fl oz. sour cream

sea salt and ground black pepper to taste

1 TBSP nutritional yeast

1 ½ tsp. konjac flour (glucomannan power)

8 oz. / 225g cheese, grated (see notes below)

12 oz. / 335g bacon, cooked and chopped

5 green onions / scallions / spring onions, thinly sliced

Steam the bite-sized cauliflower pieces until just soft. Drain very well.

Meanwhile, place the almond milk, chicken stock, cream cheese, and sour cream into a large pan over medium heat. Bring just to the boil, then reduce heat to a simmer. Stir until the cream cheese is all melted. Add the sea salt and ground black pepper and nutritional yeast and stir well.

Gently sprinkle the konjac flour over the surface of the soup while whisking rapidly with the other hand.

Add the grated cheese(s) and stir until completely melted and the soup is thickened.

Add the cooked, chopped bacon, green onions, and drained cauliflower pieces and stir until completely combined.

Serve.

~~~~~~

Top Tip: I haven't specified the type(s) of cheese here because this is one of those recipes you can have some extra fun with. I used half sharp Cheddar and half smoked gouda. Because smoked gouda is freakin' awesome in most things, and especially Mac & Cheese. Go to town and pick some exciting new cheese or mix of cheeses. You can change the cheeses up every time you make this to give you some extra variety.

The soups in this book went to my neighbors' houses for dinner. Except this one. I ate it all.

Is It Or Isn't It Chili

Prep: 15 mins | Cook: 45 mins | Total: 60 mins

2 TBSP coconut or avocado oil

8 oz. / 225g onion, finely chopped

6 cloves garlic, finely chopped

6 oz. / 170g green pepper, finely chopped

1 lb. / 450g ground (minced) beef

1 lb. / 450g cauliflower, roughly chopped

1 lb. 12 oz. / 785g canned plum tomatoes

1 tsp. sea salt

1 tsp. dried oregano

1 ½ tsp. ground coriander

3 tsp. cocoa powder

¼ tsp. ground red pepper (cayenne)

1 cup / ½ pint beef stock

½ tsp. konjac flour (glucomannan power)

½ tsp. guar gum

Melt the coconut or avocado oil over medium heat in a large pan or stock pot. Add the onion, garlic, and green pepper, and sauté until the onion is transparent, about 10 minutes.

Add the beef and continue to sauté until the meat is browned, breaking it up as it cooks.

Meanwhile, place the tomatoes and their juice in the blender, add the chopped cauliflower and blend on low speed until the cauliflower is the size of rice. Do not blend smooth!

Add the tomato and cauliflower to the beef and stir well. Add the sea salt, oregano, coriander, cocoa powder, and ground red pepper (cayenne) and mix thoroughly.

Simmer the meat mixture, uncovered, stirring often, for 30 minutes.

Put the beef stock and 1 cup of the hot meat mixture into the blender and blend on high until very smooth.

Turn the blender to low, and slowly tap the konjac flour, then the guar gum through the opening in the lid. Blend for 5 seconds.

Pour the blended stock mixture back into the pan with the meat and stir well. (cont'd next page)

Cook for a further 5 minutes to thicken, stirring often.

~~~~~~

Top Tip: Like some heat in your chili? There's about none in this. So whatever it is you add to your regular chili to make it hot – do that.

Or you could do what the gloriousness that is Rekka Jay – Graphic and Cookbook Designer for the Ketovangelist Kitchen – does and add the following with the other spices and herbs:

5 tsp. chili powder

½ tsp. cumin

4 tsp. Himalyan salt

and then top with fresh, sliced jalapenos.

~~~~~~

This is probably a good time to tell you that I have never made Chili, and I have never eaten Chili. However, you wanted Chili that was healthier, had no beans, and had way more veggies hidden in it, so I made you some. It looks like Chili, it smells like Chili, and it tastes like Chili smells.

The Soup Taste Test Crew said it was like Chili to them, and one of them said it wasn't Chili, but he loved it anyway.

Whatever you decide to call it, it's absolutely packed full of meat and veggies, plus there's a whole lot of yummy flavors going on.

Enjoy!

www.carriebrown.com

BYO (BUILD YOUR OWN) SOUPS

Sometimes, you're going to want soup that doesn't have any protein in it – either because you've reached your protein quotient for the day, or you want a bowl of something hot to go alongside a steak or juicy pork chop, or you just need fat, flavor and a warm hug.

Thus, there follows a whole bunch of meatless soups for that very purpose. However, any of these meatless soup recipes can be easily turned into a complete meal by simply adding some cooked meat – ham, chicken, and turkey all spring immediately to mind. Using these lighter meats allows the flavors of the vegetables to remain front and center, while still providing your protein fix.

The stronger meats such as ground (minced) beef, bacon, sausage, and ground (minced) pork are often best used in soups created specifically for them as they tend to outshine any other flavors around, although there are some exceptions, noted below.

Here's a cheat sheet for which meat would go best with each vegetable soup. Or, just do you.

All In A Pickle Soup	Ham	page 77
Avocado Gazpacho	Bacon	page 78
Broccoli Cheddar Soup	Ham	page 93
Cauliflower Cheese Soup	Ham	page 89
Confetti Veggie Soup	Turkey	page 88
Cream of Celery Soup	Chicken	page 96
Cream of Mushroom Soup	Chicken	page 90
Creamed Onion Soup	Sausage	page 99
Creamy Broccolini Soup	Chicken	page 91
Creamy Cucumber Soup	Ham	page 79
Cucumber, Celery and Dill Soup	Turkey	page 84
Cuke and Cauli Soup	Chicken	page 83
Green Bean Casserole Soup	Turkey	page 97
Green Pepper Leek Soup	Chicken	page 86

Leek and Cauliflower Soup	Ham	page 85
Lemon Veggie Cream Soup	Turkey	page 84
Lettuce Soup	Ham	page 102
Parsley Cream Soup	Chicken	page 100
Rosemary Asparagus Soup	Chicken	page 92
Spiced Cauliflower Soup	Chicken	page 87
Spice Pumpkin Soup	Duck	page 95
Spinach and Orange Soup	Chicken	page 101
Tomato Salad Soup	Sausage	page 81
Tomato Times Two Soup	Bacon	page 82

Make sure the meat is thoroughly cooked before adding it to the soup. In most cases you can sauté and brown the meat in the time it takes to cook the veggies in the stock. In the case of ham and pre-cooked sausage, ensure it is warmed through. An easy way to whip up a fast and highly nutritious meal!

<u>Making protein-rich soups super-fast</u>

To make meat soups super-fast, have the meat pre-cooked and stored in the 'fridge or freezer. Cook large batches of ground beef (mince), chicken, and turkey pieces, allow to cool and then bag in 1 lb. lots before labeling and freezing.

If frozen, defrost quickly while you are cooking the veggies by placing the bags of meat in the sink filled with warm water. Once defrosted, add to the soup and heat through.

I do not recommend using this method for soups containing fish. Fish is very delicate and does not stand up well to freezing once it is frozen, not to mention that it poaches so quickly you really don't need to have it ready in advance.

www.carriebrown.com

All In A Pickle Soup

Prep: 15 mins | Cook: 45 mins | Total: 60 mins

1 lb. / 450g cauliflower, roughly chopped

4 cups / 2 pints chicken stock

2 oz. / 55g butter **SUB: ghee for dairy-free**

ground black pepper

2 tsps. nutritional yeast

1 tsp. konjac flour (glucomannan power)

10 oz. / 280g dill pickles, finely chopped

½ cup / 4 fl oz. sour cream **SUB: thick coconut milk for dairy-free**

¾ cup / 6 fl oz. pickle juice (drained from jar of pickles)

sea salt to taste *optional, see instructions below

Put the cauliflower and stock in a pan over medium heat and bring to the boil. Reduce the heat and simmer for 15 minutes until the cauliflower is very soft.

Carefully transfer the cauliflower and stock to a blender, add the butter, ground black pepper, and nutritional yeast and blend on high until very smooth.

Turn the blender to low, and slowly tap the konjac flour through the opening in the lid. Blend for 5 seconds.

Pour the blended cauliflower mixture back into the pan and add the finely chopped dill pickles, sour cream, and pickle juice. Stir well until thoroughly combined.

Add sea salt to taste if required. Some pickles are saltier than others, so make sure you taste your soup before adding more salt.

Heat until warmed through and serve.

~~~~~~

If you want to know how much I love you people, want you to be Rockstars in the kitchen, and want you to have delicious KETO food to eat, look no further than this recipe.

I had never eaten a dill pickle. IN MY LIFE. Until now. But y'all were clamoring for Pickle Soup. Which required me to EAT DILL PICKLES. So I duly bought dill pickles, lovingly chopped dill pickles, added dill pickles to a perfectly lovely soup recipe and then ATE DILL PICKLES. For you. And I may even have made myself a pickle (soup) lover in the process. If you love dill pickles, you will think this soup came down from the heavens. Seattle, actually, but you won't care.

Avocado Gazpacho

Prep: 20 mins | Cook: 0 mins | Total: 20 mins

1 lb. 5 oz. / 590g English cucumber (about 1 ½), roughly chopped

4 oz. / 110g fennel, roughly chopped

5 green onions / scallions / spring onions

2 cups / 1 pint chicken stock

¾ oz. / 21g fresh basil leaves

¼ oz. / 7g fresh mint leaves

8 oz. / 225g avocado flesh (about 1 large)

2 TBSP lemon juice

2 tsp. sea salt

½ cup / 4 fl oz. heavy cream **SUB: thick coconut milk for dairy-free**

Put the chopped cucumber, fennel, green onions, stock, basil, and mint in the blender and chop on low speed. You are not trying to make it smooth, but leave it somewhat chunky. Pour the chopped veggies into a bowl.

Return 1 ½ cups of the chopped veggies to the blender, add the avocado flesh, lemon juice, sea salt, and cream and blend until very smooth. You may have to stop / start / scrape a few times as avocado can be hard to blend.

Pour the smooth avocado soup over the chopped veggies in the bowl and mix until completely combined.

Chill until ready to serve.

~~~~~~

Top Tip: If you prefer a completely smooth soup, you can blend the chopped veggies until smooth and then continue with the rest of the instructions. You may have to do the blending in two batches. The flavor will be different without the whole pieces of veggies, but it will still be delicious.

If you're looking for new ways to get your avocado in – or you don't like the texture of avocado – look no further! This delightful chilled gazpacho gives you a brilliant side to accompany your protein at mealtime, or a fantastic snack – packed with flavor, and loaded with healthy fats.

The lemon juice keeps the avocado green and gorgeous, so you can pack this in small containers and transport with you for a lunch or snack on the go. GO, avocados!

Creamy Cucumber Soup

Prep: 5 mins | Cook: 15 mins | Total: 20 mins

2 TBSP coconut oil

5 oz. / 140g (approx. 1 medium) onion, chopped

2 ½ lbs. / 1120g (approx. 3 large) English cucumbers, chopped

1½ cups / 12 fl oz. unsweetened thin coconut milk

3 tsp. sea salt

½ cup chopped fresh chives (I forgot to weigh, but it's a lot – chives are mild so you can eyeball it)

2 small avocados, skin and pits removed

2 TBSP heavy cream **SUB: thick coconut milk for dairy-free**

1 TBSP white wine

Chopped green onions (scallions or spring onions) for garnish – or more chives if you have them

In a large stock pot, sauté the onions in the coconut oil until transparent.

Add the cucumber, coconut milk and sea salt, cover and cook for 10 minutes over medium heat until cucumber is tender.

In batches, carefully transfer the cucumber and milk to a blender and blend on high until very smooth.

To the last batch, add the chives, avocado, heavy cream and white wine, and blend until completely incorporated.

Pour all batches of soup back into the stock pot, stir well, and gently re-warm if necessary.

Garnish with fresh chopped green onions (scallions).

~~~~~~

I grew up on cucumber soup. It would probably be fair to say that I've slurped down more cucumber soup than all the other soups I've ever slurped down combined. I blame this entire cucumber soup idea on my parents. My father grew cucumbers by the hundred and my mother indulged him by maniacally transforming them into soup. There were an untold number of Tupperware containers stacked in the freezer housing nothing more than cucumber soup. Unwavering was she in her use of the cucumber. It's a darn good thing we all liked her cucumber soup *as is*. This isn't that. This Creamy Cucumber Soup is something else, *entirely*.

Ah, tomatoes!

Plump, ripe, juicy, red tomatoes. Imagine yourself biting into one right now - the juice oozing down your chin, and the deeply delicious tomato flavor bursting onto your taste buds. Are you salivating yet?

I loved tomato soup when I was a kid; even though the tomato soup I grew up on came out of a packet. Looking back I realize how odd that is, since my mother made almost everything from scratch. Except soups, and a few other things like these crazy packet puddings called Angel Delight which I thought were completely magical. I dread to think what was in them – you added milk and whisked it up and put it in bowls and 30 minutes later it was thick and fluffy like a mousse. It used to set like cement in my stomach, but my mouth was so happy I didn't care. Yikes. Ignorance can seem to be bliss before one learns what's really going on in the food industry and how nutrition really affects you.

The packet soup I ate as a young 'un was mixed with water and heated; yet somehow I enjoyed it. It bears no resemblance to **real** tomato soup – you know – tomato soup with real, live tomatoes in it. All of the tomato soup recipes in this book are like tomato soup on super-steroids in comparison. In America it seems that eating Campbell's Tomato Soup is a requirement for a happy life. These recipes ain't nothing like Campbell's, either. If you think that Campbell's tastes "Mmm, mmm….good!" just wait until you get your first spoonful of any of these down your gullet. Then come back and talk to me about "Mmm, mmm….good!"

While we are on the subject of tomatoes, I thought I should mention that – in case anyone is wondering – I didn't purchase any particular type of tomatoes for these recipes. Just between you and me, I purchased whatever type were the cheapest per pound when I was eagerly gathering soup-making produce at the store. I am clearly not a tomato snob; well not when it comes to soup, anyway. When I am eating them raw I do have a penchant for those gorgeous little cherry tomatoes, packed with so much flavor your mouth barely knows what to do with itself. But soup? Sometimes I use plum, sometimes vine, sometimes cherry. Beefsteak, heirloom, globe. I am not fussy. And sometimes, if I am feeling particularly rambunctious, I'll toss in any combination of any of the above.

The only time I'm specific is when it comes to canned plum tomatoes, because raw tomatoes just don't taste anything quite like those, and some recipes just scream for the uniqueness that only they bring to the proceedings.

With all that said, however, just be careful with your tomato consumption since they do contain natural sugars, and too much can push your carbs up. Don't go crazy, and don't tomato too often. Unless you know that tomatoes don't affect you, in which case – have at 'em!

Whatever type is your favorite, GO tomatoes!

Tomato Salad Soup

Prep: 10 mins | Cook: 15 mins | Total: 25 mins

1 lb. 11 oz. / 760g (approx. 2 large) English cucumbers, roughly chopped

1 lb. / 450g tomatoes, roughly chopped

1 cup / 8 fl oz. chicken stock

2 tsp. sea salt

3 tsp. dried basil

4 oz. / 110g unsweetened tomato paste

1 small avocado, peeled and pitted

3 TBSP white wine

2 tsp. lemon juice

2 TBSP Full Fat Greek yogurt (Do not use non-fat – it will separate) **SUB: thick coconut milk for dairy-free**

1 large head Romaine lettuce

Put the cucumber, tomatoes, stock, sea salt, and basil into a large pan or stock pot, bring to the boil, then simmer, covered, for 15 minutes until the vegetables are soft.

Working in batches, place the vegetables in a blender and blend until very smooth.

To the last batch, add the tomato paste, avocado flesh, white wine, lemon juice and Greek yogurt, and blend to mix.

Separate the leaves of the lettuce and one-by-one, passing through the hole in the blender lid, blend into the soup on high speed until completely smooth.

Pour all batches of soup back into the stock pot, stir well, and gently re-warm if necessary.

~~~~~~

One day I peered into the depths of my 'fridge and surveyed the contents, looking for something that could be made warm and tasty in a very short time. When all I could find was ingredients for salad, I was all kinds of disappointed. As soon as the leaves turn, I want warm. So I started to wonder what would happen if I turned all that salad stuff into soup – all together at the same time. This is what happens: Tomato Salad Soup. Need to eat salad in winter but want something hot to stave off the cold? This is all the goodness of salad made warm and tasty. In the first iteration I even squirted in some mayonnaise. I do not recommend this. AT ALL. Please do not do this at home. It was not good. AT ALL. The second iteration, on the other hand, was a huge hit.

Tomato Times Two Soup

Prep: 10 mins | Cook: 15 mins | Total: 25 mins

2 cups / 1 pint chicken stock

8 oz. / 225g celery, roughly chopped

4 oz. / 110g tomato purée / paste

2 lbs. / 900g plum tomatoes, roughly chopped

3 tsp. dried basil

3 TBSP dry white wine

6 TBSP Full Fat Greek yogurt (Do not use non-fat – it will separate) **SUB: thick coconut milk for dairy-free**

½ tsp. sea salt

ground black pepper to taste

3 oz. / 85g spinach

1 tsp. guar gum

Place stock, celery, tomato paste, tomatoes, and basil in a large pan or stock pot and bring to the boil. Reduce the heat, cover, and simmer for about 10 minutes until the tomatoes and celery are very soft.

Working in batches, place the vegetables in a blender and blend until very smooth.

To the last batch, add the basil, wine, Greek yogurt, sea salt, pepper, and spinach. Blend just until the spinach has disappeared.

Turn the blender to low and slowly tap the guar gum through the opening in the lid. Blend for 5 seconds.

Pour all batches of soup back into the stock pot, stir well, and gently re-warm if necessary.

~~~~~~

If you love tomatoes, this soup packs some serious tomato punch. Plus spinach that you don't even know is there when you eat it.

It was a totally tomato weekend back when I threw this extravagantly rich tomato-fest together for you. While I was reading labels on cans of tomato purée at the grocery store – with this soup in mind – I got inspired to make those Tomato Basil Biscuits at the back of this book. That same weekend I also conjured up the very popular Tomato Salad Soup, aka How to Eat Salad Greens without Having to Eat Salad Greens. I also learned which sun-dried tomato, which tomato paste, and which tomato purée brands are unsweetened. *Always* good to know.

Cuke and Cauli Soup

Prep: 10 mins | Cook: 15 mins | Total: 25 mins

2 cups / 1 pint chicken stock

1lb 8 oz. / 670g (approx. 1 medium) cauliflower, roughly chopped

2lb 8 oz. / 1120g (approx. 3 large) English cucumber, roughly chopped

3 oz. / 85g butter **SUB: ghee for dairy-free**

1 TBSP chopped fresh mint

1 tsp. sea salt

4 oz. / 110g fresh spinach

Place the stock, cauliflower, and cucumber in a large pan or stock pot and bring to the boil. Reduce the heat, cover, and simmer for about 15 minutes, until the vegetables are very soft.

Working in batches, place the vegetables in a blender and blend until very smooth. It may take a while.

To the last batch, add the butter, mint, sea salt, and spinach. Blend just until the spinach has disappeared.

Pour all batches of soup back into the stock pot, stir well, and gently re-warm if necessary.

~~~~~~

I have slurped down hundreds of gallons of cucumber soup in my life – most all of it while sitting at my parents dining room table in England, and most all of it made with cucumbers grown in my father's greenhouse. My father was the Cucumber King, back in the day, and my mother couldn't keep up with the supply, despite my eating the things as if they were dark green, ridiculously juicy, elongated apples. I still eat them like apples today, much to the amusement of the folks that I work with. Every day, at some point, I can be found gnawing at a whole English cucumber.

These cucumber soups I've made for you – I think you'll like them. I really hope you do.

I think you'll be really surprised by how fantastical a cucumber can taste. Throw away all thoughts of crisp, watery and cold. Think smooth, warm, creamy and even slightly sweet. Instead of boycotting the lovely cucumber until summer rolls back around, invite her in for the winter; although if you're somewhere warm right now, make these soups and then chill them and enjoy them cold. Either way, hot or cold, you can now get some major cucumber-y goodness inside you without having to eat a salad. Hurrah!

Cucumber, Celery and Dill Soup

Prep: 10 mins | Cook: 15 mins | Total: 25 mins

2 cups / 1 pint chicken stock

2 ½ lbs. / 1120g (approx. 3 large) English cucumbers, roughly chopped

8 oz. / 225g celery, roughly chopped

½ cup / 4 fl oz. thick coconut milk

¾ tsp. sea salt

2 tsp. fresh chopped dill

3 tsp. lime juice

½ tsp. konjac flour (glucomannan powder)

½ tsp. guar gum

Put the stock, cucumbers and celery in a large pan or stock pot over medium heat, cover, and simmer until the vegetables are soft – about 15 minutes.

Working in batches, place the vegetables in a blender and blend until very smooth. Don't give up! Keep blending! Smoothness shall be yours!

To the last batch add the coconut milk, sea salt, dill, and lime juice, and blend until completely mixed.

Turn the blender to low and slowly tap the konjac flour and then the guar gum through the opening in the lid. Blend for 5 seconds.

Pour all batches of soup back into the stock pot, stir well, and gently re-warm if necessary.

~~~~~~

If my fellow Americans are wondering why I always specify English cucumbers in my recipes, here's why English cucumbers are awesome:

- They're bigger. Now there's a first!
- The seeds are smaller and so soft you don't notice them.
- They are not bitter tasting.
- The skin is not tough and they don't need to be peeled. We love less peeling!
- They're sweeter and have more flavor.
- They are prettier when sliced or chopped. I'm serious. Attractive food is important.
- They are cheap as chips at Costco, like 3 for 2 bucks.

GO, English cucumbers!!

www.carriebrown.com

Leek and Cauliflower Soup

Prep: 10 mins | Cook: 15 mins | Total: 25 mins

4 cups / 2 pints chicken stock

¾ cup / 6 fl oz. white cooking wine

1 ½ lbs. / 670g leeks (use it all!), roughly chopped

2 lbs. / 900g cauliflower, cut into small pieces

2 tsp. dried spearmint or peppermint

1 tsp. dried rosemary

1 tsp. sea salt

3 oz. / 85g butter **SUB: ghee for dairy-free**

Heat the chicken stock and white cooking wine in a large pan or stockpot.

Add leeks and cauliflower, spearmint, rosemary and salt to the stockpot.

Cover and simmer until cauliflower is just tender.

Working in batches, blend the vegetables on high until they are completely smooth.

To the last batch, add the butter and blend.

Pour all batches of soup back into the stock pot, stir well, and gently re-warm if necessary.

~~~~~~

If you've been reading my blog or listening to our podcasts for any length of time, you'll know that I think leeks are the finest vegetable on earth. This probably accounts for the all of recipes in this cookbook involving leeks. Leeks rock.

If you haven't ever tried leeks, I urge you to embrace them wholeheartedly the next time you are in the produce section of your grocery store. They look like enormous green (spring) onions – the white root end being about 1 ½" thick. In most recipes you'll be advised to only use the white part, but in soups – since you're probably going to blend the living daylights out of them – I thoroughly recommend using the whole leek, green bits and all. Just top and tail before you started chopping and get the most bang for your leeky buck.

Once you've realized how very awesome leeks are, head on over to www.carriebrown.com, go to the blog, type "leeks" in the search box, and you'll find all sorts of other delicious leekery going on.

If you're doing *very* low carb you may want to avoid a lot of leeks until you're closer to goal.

Green Pepper Leek Soup

Prep: 10 mins | Cook: 20 mins | Total: 30 mins

3 cups / 1 ½ pints chicken stock

2 lbs. / 900g leeks, roughly chopped

7 oz. / 200g (approx.1 large) green pepper

1 tsp. sea salt

4 oz. / 110g butter **SUB: ghee for dairy-free**

ground black pepper to taste

1 TBSP lemon juice

2 TBSP chopped fresh thyme

4 oz. / 110g fresh spinach

Heat the chicken stock, leeks, and green pepper in a large pan or stock pot, cover, and simmer for about 15 minutes until the vegetables are very soft.

Working in batches, blend the vegetables on high until they are completely smooth. It will take a while, and that's OK.

To the last batch, add the sea salt, butter, pepper, lemon juice, thyme, and spinach, and blend just until the spinach disappears.

Pour all batches of soup back into the stock pot, stir well, and gently re-warm if necessary.

~~~~~~

There's a few recipes in this cookbook that have a whole bunch of spinach hiding in them. I am not talking about the recipes where spinach is clearly the star of the show. I am talking about the recipes where other veggies take center stage, and spinach slides in through the side stage door at the last minute. There's quite a few of those in here – this recipe being one of them.

Why? Leafy greens are all kinds of good for us, so I take every opportunity that I can to cram them into every nook and cranny of your meals without you having the feeling that various forms of leafy greenery is the only food you eat. While we want the benefits of eating a lot of greens, our taste buds don't want to think that's all they're getting.

Why do we add the spinach last? If you eat raw spinach in salads you'll know that it really doesn't taste of much until you cook it. By adding the spinach last – and not cooking it – you can't detect it in the soup; this lets the other veggies continue to shine in the flavor department, while getting all the added goodness that those leafy greens bring to the table. Everyone wins.

If you're doing *very* low carb you may want to avoid a lot of leeks until you're closer to goal.

Spiced Cauliflower Soup

Prep: 10 mins | Cook: 15 mins | Total: 25 mins

2 cups / 1 pint chicken stock

1 ½ lbs. / 670 g (approx. 1 medium) cauliflower, cut into florets

7 oz. / 195g (approx. 1 medium) onion, chopped

1 tsp. sea salt

½ cup / 4 fl oz. heavy cream **SUB: thick coconut milk for dairy-free**

½ tsp. Five Spice (do not guess, it's powerful)

1 tsp. lemon juice

Put the stock, cauliflower and onion in a stock pot over a medium heat, cover, and cook for 15 minutes until cauliflower is tender.

Working in batches, carefully transfer vegetables and stock to a blender.

Blend on high until completely smooth.

To the last batch, add salt, cream, five spice, and lemon juice and blend for another minute.

Pour all batches of soup back into the stock pot, stir well, and gently re-warm if necessary.

~~~~~~

For years cauliflower has always been the bridesmaid and never the bride; because cauliflower just steamed and plonked on a plate is really rather bland.

So one day I elected cauliflower as the star of my next soup recipe, because I wanted to surprise you with a wholeheartedly exciting cauliflower soup. One that might allow you see the bashful cauliflower in a whole new light. I browsed around the herb and spice department for quite some time – trying to imagine what various combinations could do to a humble cauliflower's street cred – before my gaze alighted on the canister full of Five Spice. Hands up if you've only ever had Five Spice with chicken? Me! Me! Pick me! I decided it was high time for Five Spice to infiltrate other areas of my culinary adventures, and high time for cauliflower to shine.

This soup is a cinch to throw together and extremely filling. It is creamy and comforting like potato soup; and it goes brilliantly with those Cheesy Biscuits (see page 103) everyone gets so excited about.

So without further ado, here's my Spiced Cauliflower Soup for you. GO, cauliflower!!

Confetti Veggie Soup

Prep: 10 mins | Cook: 25 mins | Total: 35 mins

3 cups / 1 ½ pints chicken stock

1 lb. / 450g cauliflower florets

1 cup / 8 fl oz. water

6 oz. / 170g celery, roughly chopped

7 oz. / 200g onion, roughly chopped

5 oz. / 140g red pepper, de-seeded and roughly chopped

5 oz. / 140g green pepper, de-seeded and roughly chopped

2 oz. / 55g butter **SUB: ghee for dairy-free**

1 tsp. sea salt

ground black pepper to taste

½ cup / 4 fl oz. heavy cream **SUB: thick coconut milk for dairy-free**

¾ tsp. guar gum

12 sprigs fresh flat leaf parsley

Put the stock and cauliflower in a stock pot, cover, and cook for 15 minutes until cauliflower is very soft.

Meanwhile, in a separate pan, place the water, celery, onion, red and green pepper, and cook over a medium heat until crisp-tender – about 10 minutes.

Once cauliflower is very soft, blend with the stock, butter, sea salt, pepper, and cream until very smooth.

Turn the blender to low, and slowly tap the guar gum through the opening in the lid.

Add the crisp-tender veggies and parsley to the cauliflower puree in the blender and blend on the lowest possible speed so the veggies do not get blended smooth. Leave the veggies as lumpy as you like. Return the soup to the pan and gently warm if necessary.

~~~~~~

Why I never made soup with lumpy bits in, long before I embarked on this soup cookbook writing escapade, is a mystery to me. This soup is the bomb. Never have I enjoyed a mixed vegetable soup as much as this one. And here's the kicker: if it was blended until it was smooth, you wouldn't be able to taste all the different flavors. It's like vegetable confetti being sprinkled in your mouth. YUM.

Cauliflower Cheese Soup

Prep: 10 mins | Cook: 20 mins | Total: 30mins

1 ½ lbs. / 670g cauliflower, roughly chopped

3 cups / 1 ½ pints chicken stock

¼ cup / 2 fl oz. heavy cream

½ tsp. sea salt

Ground black pepper to taste

2 oz. / 55g butter

½ tsp. konjac flour (glucomannan powder)

5 oz. / 140g Sharp (strong) Cheddar cheese

Place the cauliflower and stock in a large pan or stock pot, covered, over medium heat and simmer until just tender, about 15 minutes. Do not overcook! You'll have mushy soup and you'll be sad.

Transfer the cauliflower and stock to the blender, and add the cream, sea salt, pepper, and butter.

Blend on the lowest possible speed to keep the cauliflower with a lot of texture. You do not want puree.

With the blender still on low, slowly tap the konjac flour through the opening in the lid, and blend for 5 seconds.

Return the soup to the pan and warm over the lowest heat. Add the grated cheese and stir until completely melted through the soup.

~~~~~~

Top Tip: Cut the cauliflower lengthwise through the stem when chopping. This makes the cauliflower cook quicker and more evenly.

Cauliflower Cheese is one of my childhood all-time favorite food memories; along with Sainsbury's Steak and Kidney Pie and crinkle-cut chips (fries), and anything topped with mashed potatoes, or smothered in cheese sauce. And when I say cheese sauce, I am not referring to anything that comes out of a tube, a container of any kind, and / or glows in the dark.

When I asked my Roomie what she thought of the Cauliflower Cheese Soup she said, "It makes me think of a long, cold, winter night, a warm fireplace, and a steaming bowl of comfort food."

Cream of Mushroom Soup

Prep: 10 mins | Cook: 10 mins | Total: 20mins

2 TBSP coconut oil

6 cloves garlic, crushed

1 ½ lb. / 670g mushrooms

3 cups / 1 ½ pints beef stock

½ cup / 4 fl oz. heavy cream **SUB: thick coconut milk for dairy-free**

1 tsp. sea salt

1 tsp. guar gum

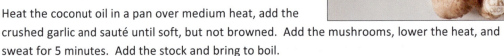

Heat the coconut oil in a pan over medium heat, add the crushed garlic and sauté until soft, but not browned. Add the mushrooms, lower the heat, and sweat for 5 minutes. Add the stock and bring to boil.

Using a slotted spoon, carefully remove half the mushrooms into a bowl and reserve.

Transfer the remaining mushrooms and stock to the blender, add the cream and sea salt, and blend like mad until smooth.

Turn the blender to low, and slowly tap the guar gum through the opening in the lid.

Add the reserved mushrooms and pulse a few times on the lowest possible speed to keep the mushrooms with a lot of texture. Warm gently if necessary.

~~~~~~

I have a love for mushrooms that runs very, very deep. In my little world, much like bacon, mushrooms make everything better. Except maybe oatmeal, but since I no longer eat oats, it's really not a problem of any great magnitude.

The best Mushroom Soup I've ever had the pleasure of slurping down was in Jukkasjärvi, Swedish Lapland, way up there in the Arctic Circle. I cannot imagine where they got mushrooms in the middle of a -40ºC winter, but they sure knew what to do with them once they got their mitts on some. My eyes flew open as wide as saucers the moment the first spoonful slipped past my lips. I could have eaten that soup every day for the rest of my life and never tired of it.

If you really want to pimp your Mushroom Soup, use any combination of fancy mushrooms that you can get your hands on at the store, or soak some dried wild mushrooms overnight, drain well and use as fresh mushrooms to make your soup the next day. Mushroom nirvana will be yours.

Creamy Broccolini Soup

Prep: 10 mins | Cook: 15 mins | Total: 25mins

1 lb. / 450g broccolini, roughly chopped – stalks and all!

8 oz. / 225g cauliflower florets, roughly chopped

4 cups / 2 pints of vegetable stock

2 tsp. sea salt

Ground black pepper to taste

½ cup / 4 fl oz. heavy cream **SUB: extra coconut milk for dairy-free**

¼ cup / 2 fl oz. thick coconut milk

1 tsp. lemon juice

2 oz. / 55g fresh spinach

Place the broccolini, cauliflower and stock in a large pan or stock pot over a medium heat and bring to the boil. Cover and simmer until the vegetables are soft, about 15 minutes.

Working in batches, transfer the veggies and stock to a blender and blend until very smooth.

To the last batch add the sea salt, pepper, cream, coconut milk, and lemon juice.

Add the spinach and blend just until it disappears.

Pour all batches of soup back into the stock pot, stir well, and gently re-warm if necessary.

~~~~~~

I was a bit confused on the whole broccolini thing. Even the spell checker was confused about it. Well, it might not be confused, but it certainly doesn't know how to spell it. To me broccolini just looks like broccoli with extra-long stalks and fluffier florets. But a lady that I work with, when asked what her 3 favorite soups were, said, "Anything with broccolini. I love broccolini."

Always open to a bit of education, I discovered that "broccolini" is a registered trademark of Mann Packing Co., and that the vegetable known as "broccolini" is a hybrid of broccoli and kai-lan, which is Chinese broccoli. So I was right. It's broccoli with extra-long stalks and fluffier florets. Oh, and it's good for you. We can now remove our "broccolini" training wheels. I think, however, that the spell checker is still confused. There's always one.

Rosemary Asparagus Soup

Prep: 10 mins | Cook: 15 mins | Total: 25 mins

3 cups / 1 ½ pints chicken stock

1 ½ lbs. / 670g asparagus

9 oz. / 250g cauliflower

2 oz. / 55g butter **SUB: ghee for dairy-free**

1 tsp. sea salt

¼ cup / 4 fl oz. heavy cream **SUB: thick coconut milk for dairy-free**

½ tsp. chopped fresh rosemary

½ tsp. guar gum

Place the stock, asparagus, and cauliflower in a large pan or stock pot over a medium heat and bring to the boil. Cover and simmer until the vegetables are soft, about 15 minutes.

Working in batches, carefully transfer the stock and vegetables to a blender.

Blend the stock and veggies a *lot* – and I really mean a *lot* – until completely smooth.

Pass the soup through a fine mesh sieve to remove any asparagus fibers. You'll be amazed at how many fibers you catch!

Pour half of the soup back into the blender and add the butter, sea salt, cream, and rosemary. Blend until thoroughly mixed.

Turn the blender to low, and slowly tap the guar gum through the opening in the lid. Blend for 5 seconds.

Pour all batches of soup back into the stock pot, stir well, and gently re-warm if necessary.

~~~~~~

There's a surprising amount of woody bits in even fresh, young asparagus, which I am guessing you don't want in your soup. Therefore, I highly recommend you taking the time to pass it through a sieve after blending it. Unless you especially like the sensation of finding a hair in your soup, in which case – be my guest – you'll have plenty of "hair" moments in just one small bowlful.

I confess I prefer my asparagus lightly steamed and dripping with butter, but this dreamy, creamy delicately flavored soup comes in a close second! Hot or cold, a fantastic way to get your asparagus on.

Broccoli Cheddar Soup

Prep: 10 mins | Cook: 20 mins | Total: 30 mins

2 tsp. konjac flour (glucomannan powder)

4 cups / 2 pints chicken stock, divided

1 cup / 8 fl oz. thick coconut milk

½ cup / 4 fl oz. heavy cream

1 ½ lbs. / 670g broccoli florets

1 ½ tsp. sea salt

Ground black pepper to taste

½ tsp. ground cloves

2 TBSP balsamic vinegar

8 oz. / 225g sharp (strong) cheddar cheese

Place the konjac flour in a bowl and while whisking rapidly, add 1 cup / 8 fl oz. of the stock. Whisk until the konjac is completely dispersed.

Put the remaining 3 cups / 1 ½ pints stock, coconut milk, cream, and broccoli in a large pan or stock pot over a medium heat. Pour in the konjac flour and stock mixture and stir well.

Bring to the boil and then reduce heat to simmer for 15 minutes until broccoli is just tender. Do not overcook! No one likes mushy broccoli.

Once the broccoli is just tender, remove from the heat and stir in the sea salt, pepper, ground cloves, and balsamic vinegar.

Use a masher or an immersion blender to break up the broccoli florets a little. If you use an immersion blender, "pulse" it so you don't end up smashing the broccoli into mush. No one likes mushy broccoli. I think I mentioned that earlier. I still maintain it is true.

Add the grated cheese and stir until completely melted through the soup.

~~~~~~

Ah! Broccoli Cheddar Soup. One of those beloved American classics that appears on diner and chain-restaurant menus from sea to shining sea; not to mention popping up on just about every American's soup wish-list. It's not something I had ever eaten until I arrived stateside, and between you and me, it's not a dish that I have embraced. Give me Cauliflower Cheese Soup over Broccoli Cheddar any day. But since I had more requests for Broccoli Cheddar Soup than any other – I lovingly made this for Americans all over this magnificent lump of land.

Lemon Veggie Cream Soup

Prep: 10 mins | Cook: 25 mins | Total: 35mins

2 TBSP coconut or avocado oil

4 oz. / 110g celery, roughly chopped

7 oz. / 200g onion, roughly chopped

3 oz. / 85g broccoli, roughly chopped

4 cups / 2 pints chicken stock

1 lemon

1 tsp. sea salt

¼ cup / 2 fl oz. heavy cream **SUB: thick coconut milk for dairy-free**

½ oz. snipped fresh chives

½ tsp. konjac flour (glucomannan powder)

½ tsp. guar gum

Heat the coconut or avocado oil in a large pan or stock pot over medium heat, add the celery, onion, and broccoli, and sauté for about 10 minutes until veggies are crisp-tender.

Add the stock, lemon rind and juice, and bring to the boil. Reduce heat, cover, and simmer for 15 minutes.

Transfer to a blender and add the sea salt, cream and chives.

Blend on the lowest speed just until mixed thoroughly. This will keep the veggies in pieces.

Keeping the blender on low, slowly tap the konjac flour and then the guar gum through the opening in the lid just until mixed through.

~~~~~~

Top Tip: If you're looking for a great base for some leftover chicken (or turkey) – this soup would be ideal. Shred or chop up some cooked poultry, sauté gently to warm through, and toss into the finished soup. Chicken and lemon have always been best friends in the kitchen, and adding some here would give you a perfect, portable hot or cold lunch.

As good as this lusciously creamy, lemony soup is warm, it would be equally delicious chilled in the summer months. It's bright and fresh, and will make your mouth sparkle. The idea came from an old English recipe that I found hidden in one of my beloved, battered cookbooks that I've hauled around the world with me. An oldie but goodie!

Spiced Pumpkin Soup

Prep: 5 mins | Cook: 5 mins | Total: 10 mins

3 cups / 1 ½ pints chicken stock

30 oz. / 840g (2 cans) pumpkin (nothing else added, just schmushed pumpkin)

1 tsp. fresh chopped sage

1 tsp. fresh chopped rosemary

½ tsp. sea salt

¼ tsp. white pepper

¼ tsp. nutmeg

¼ cup / 2 fl oz. heavy cream **SUB: thick coconut milk for dairy-free**

1 oz. / 30g butter **SUB: ghee for dairy-free**

½ tsp. guar gum

In a large pan heat the stock and pumpkin over a medium heat until just beginning to boil.

Remove from the heat and transfer to a blender. Blend it on high. A lot.

Add the sage, rosemary, sea salt, pepper, nutmeg, cream, and butter.

Blend it a lot more. Then, if you want it really smooth and creamy, blend it just a little bit more.

Turn the blender to low, and slowly tap the guar gum through the opening in the lid. Blend for 5 seconds.

~~~~~~

This must be the fastest soup in history. If you have canned pumpkin, stock and a bunch of seasonings on hand, you can have a fantastically warming, filling meal ready in 10 minutes. GO, pumpkin! If you prefer to use fresh pumpkin, go ahead. Just don't ask me how big a pumpkin you need or how to do it. I have never touched a real, live pumpkin IN MY LIFE. True story.

In England we think pumpkins are strange, orange, grooved globes that Americans cut faces into for Halloween. I'm not even sure we think they're edible. OK, maybe things have changed since I wandered off westwards over a decade ago, but certainly, when I was a nipper, pumpkins were what Cinderella rode to the ball in, not something you'd eat.

However, you asked for Pumpkin Soup and I am here to serve. I hope you don't mind that I spiced it up a little. I promise there'll be no golden gown and glass slippers.

Cream of Celery Soup

Prep: 10 mins | Cook: 20 mins | Total: 30 mins

3 cups / 1 ½ pints chicken stock

1lb 12 oz. / 785g celery, roughly chopped

10 oz. / 280g cauliflower, roughly chopped

1 tsp. sea salt

1 TBSP fresh, chopped sage

½ cup / 4 fl oz. heavy cream **SUB: thick coconut milk for dairy-free**

½ tsp. konjac flour (glucomannan powder)

½ tsp. guar gum

Put the stock, celery, and cauliflower in a stock pot, cover, and simmer for 20 minutes until the veggies are very soft.

Transfer the stock and veggies to the blender and blend the living daylights out of it. When you think it's done, blend it for another 2 minutes. It needs to be seriously smooth.

Add the sea salt, sage, and cream, and blend to mix.

Turn the blender to low, and slowly tap the konjac flour and then the guar gum through the opening in the lid. Blend for 5 seconds.

~~~~~~

I. LOVE. THIS. SOUP.

I don't even care for celery that much, but simmer it until soft, add some fresh sage and cream, and magical, magical things happen to it. Truly.

Growing up I was fascinated by my father's on-going celery habit. My mother would ceremoniously place an entire celery heart upright in a glass in front of his place setting at the dinner table. I would studiously watch as he dipped the ends in salt before munching his way through the whole lot. No one else ever got a glass of celery, but I have no answer for you as to why. I was force-fed spinach, but never celery. Who knows. Parents are funny.

Top Tip: Sauté a pound of fresh ground sausage (sausage meat) in a skillet, drain it well, and stir it into the finished soup for a delicious protein-packed version that will keep you on the go all day, or make a perfect quick and tasty dinner on a busy evening, especially if the soup has been made ahead of time: warm the soup while you're sautéing the sausage...done!

Green Bean Casserole Soup

Prep: 10 mins | Cook: 30 mins | Total: 40 mins

1 lb. / 450g trimmed green beans, chopped into 1" pieces

10 oz. / 280g onion, roughly chopped

2 TBSP coconut oil

8 oz. / 225g mushrooms, roughly chopped

2 cups / 1 pint chicken stock

½ cup / 4 fl oz. heavy cream **SUB: thick coconut milk for dairy-free**

1 tsp. sea salt

Ground black pepper to taste

¼ tsp. celery salt

½ tsp. konjac flour (glucomannan powder)

½ tsp. guar gum

Steam the green beans until just crisp-tender. Drain well – because no one likes soggy beans.

Meanwhile, sauté the onion in the coconut oil for about 10 minutes, until transparent. Add the mushrooms and sauté for a further 5 minutes.

Add the stock, cream, sea salt, pepper and celery salt, bring to the boil and cook for 1 minute.

Transfer the soup to the blender and blend briefly on the lowest speed so that the onion and mushrooms stay in pieces.

With the blender still on low, slowly tap the konjac flour and then the guar gum through the opening in the lid. Blend for 5 seconds.

Pour the soup back into the pan and stir in the reserved green beans, and gently re-warm if necessary.

~~~~~~

Oh, Green Bean Casserole. For non-Americans, Green Bean Casserole is green beans mixed with condensed cream of mushroom soup, piled into a baking dish and garnished with a can of crispy store-bought onion rings. Yes you read that right. Americans LOVE it with their Thanksgiving Dinner. The first (and only) time I ate it I thought it was the strangest side dish ever. I pretty much still do. I thought it would be fun to make a soup version that's way better for you and that you can enjoy all year round. The onions aren't crispy, and it's all made from scratch, but it tastes delicious ☺

I've always been a veggie girl, and I have my parents to thank for that. I grew up knowing that vegetables were awesome things to eat, and excepting spinach, there really wasn't a veggie alive that I didn't like. These days I have added spinach to my list of loves, and kale to the *not so much* list, although paired with enough sausages I'll even happily munch some of that down. I particularly love vegetables that are new to a lot of Americans – leeks, parsnips, rutabaga (swede), beets (beetroot) – so much so that I was once introduced to a group of people, "This is Carrie Brown. She favors strange vegetables." BEST. INTRO. EVER.

I consider myself very lucky to have lived in a home where my father grew all sorts of vegetables in our garden, and my mother knew how to cook them so that they still tasted like they were supposed to. There were no mushy, tasteless veggie offerings at our house. Brussels Sprouts were sweet, tender and bright green, cauliflower held its shape and didn't arrive at the table as a mushy grey mess, and carrots didn't disintegrate when you jabbed them with your fork. We got to eat veggies how they were intended to be. It wasn't that we ate huge amounts of them, but what we did eat were fresh, well-cooked and tasty. In the summer we ate huge main course salads on Sunday. I loved those Sundays.

If I'm picking favorites, anyone who has read my blog or listened to our podcasts will know *for sure* that leeks are my favorites. I am very partial to parsnips, but rarely indulge these days since they are not the healthiest option, being pretty starchy.

As a veggie-loving girl I have been amazed at how I love veggies even more since I embarked on this cookbook. I was stunned at how veggies can be made to taste completely different depending on the other ingredients or the cooking method involved. I have discovered that I now love veggies I didn't think I particularly cared for – celery springs immediately to mind. I believe I would be correct if I said I have eaten more celery in the last several months of cookbook-writing than in the rest of my life combined.

The humble cauliflower, once reserved only for a piping hot dish of Cauliflower Cheese, has proven to be one of the MVPs of the vegetable world. I even found a way to love eating green beans. And let's not forget that my love-hate relationship with kale has now blossomed into a new romance. Who knew?!

Developing these recipes has changed my world, one nutritious vegetable at a time.

~~~~~~

Cucumber soup love:

Lorrie Heist – "Some friends and I got together for a taste-testing party with all of Carrie's soups shared on her blog, www.carriebrown.com . My favorite was the Creamy Cucumber Soup. I love cucumbers, but never thought of blending cucumbers into a soup. I was hooked with the first taste! I've made this soup several times and it is so easy to prepare and package up for an upcoming busy week. It's a great way to add veggies to your meals!!"

www.carriebrown.com

Creamed Onion Soup

Prep: 10 mins | Cook: 20 mins | Total: 30 mins

2 TBSP coconut oil

1lb 10 oz. / 730g onions, roughly chopped

2 ½ cups / 1 pint, 4 fl oz. chicken stock

1 cup / 8 fl oz. thick coconut milk

½ cup / 4 fl oz. heavy cream **SUB: thick coconut milk for dairy-free**

1 ½ tsp. sea salt

Ground black pepper to taste

¾ tsp. ground nutmeg

2 tsp. onion powder

½ tsp. konjac flour (glucomannan powder)

½ tsp. guar gum

Heat the coconut oil in a large pan or stock pot over medium heat and sauté the onions until they are transparent – about 10 minutes.

Add the stock, cover, and simmer for 10 minutes.

Transfer the onions and stock to the blender, add the coconut milk, cream, sea salt, pepper, nutmeg, and onion powder, and blend briefly on the lowest speed so that the onions stay in pieces. Everyone will think you spent hours crying over a bucket of onions in order to get those beautiful small dice.

With the blender still on low, slowly tap the konjac flour and then the guar gum through the opening in the lid. Blend for 5 seconds.

~~~~~~

One of the great things about this Creamy Onion Soup is that you don't have to spend a whole bunch of time dicing the onions to make them look pretty – let the blender do the work for you. Cut the root off, peel the skin back, chop, chop, chop, and into the pot they go. No tears required. We love that.

Top Tip: Onions take on a whole new flavor and mellowness when they've been sautéed and softened and teased into tender, transparent morsels. I used regular white onions for this recipe, and you should too if you want the lowest carb option. Yellow onions are also good; sweet and red onions not so much. If you like your onions very mild, you might experiment with half the onion powder, or none at all.

Parsley Cream Soup

Prep: 10 mins | Cook: 20 mins | Total: 30 mins

2 TBSP coconut oil

3 oz. / 85g celery, roughly chopped

6 oz. / 170g onion, roughly chopped

4 oz. / 110g parsley – it's a lot, see note below

4 cups / 2 pints chicken stock

½ tsp. sea salt

Ground black pepper to taste

½ cup / 4 fl oz. thick coconut milk

1 oz. / 30g butter **SUB: ghee for dairy-free**

2 tsp. lemon juice

1 tsp. konjac flour (glucomannan powder)

1 tsp. guar gum

Heat the coconut oil over medium heat in a large pan or stock pot; add the celery, onion, and parsley, cover, and sauté for about 15 minutes until parsley is completely wilted and veggies soft.

Add the stock to the veggies and bring to the boil.

Transfer the stock and veggies to the blender, add the sea salt, pepper, coconut milk, butter, and lemon juice, and blend on high until it is very smooth. NOTE: You will never get the parsley completely smooth and blended in. Accept it and move on. Besides, it makes the soup look awful pretty.

Turn the blender to low, and slowly tap the konjac flour and then the guar gum through the opening in the lid. Blend for 5 seconds.

~~~~~~

What does 4 oz. of parsley look like? If you're in the US I'm sure you've seen the huge bunches of parsley at the grocery store for a buck. That'll give you 4 oz. of sprigs to work with. Make sure you pick it over before you throw it in the pot - there's often wilty bits hiding in the middle, and I know you don't want those in your soup. Remove the sprigs from the long stems and you'll be good to go.

Parsley is all kinds of brilliant for us. Give your body a fantastically tasty tonic today!

Spinach and Orange Soup

Prep: 10 mins | Cook: 30 mins | Total: 40 mins

2 TBSP coconut oil

1 ½ lbs. / 670g fresh spinach

13 oz. / 365g onions, roughly chopped

Rind of 2 oranges

2 cups / 1 pint chicken stock

1 ½ tsp. sea salt

Ground black pepper to taste

½ cup / 4 fl oz. thick coconut milk

1 tsp. orange extract

½ cup / 4 fl oz. heavy cream **SUB: thick coconut milk for dairy-free**

½ tsp. guar gum

Heat the coconut oil in a large pan or stock pot, and sauté the spinach and onions over medium heat until the spinach has completely wilted – about 10 minutes.

Add the orange rind and stock to the pan, cover, and cook for 20 minutes.

Transfer the veggies and stock to the blender and blend well until super smooth. Add the sea salt, pepper, coconut milk, orange extract, and cream and blend to mix.

Turn the blender to low, and slowly tap the guar gum through the opening in the lid. Blend for 5 seconds.

~~~~~~

My first recollection of spinach was dark green and slimy, with the taste of old socks. I grew up thinking that spinach was square, because the only way I ever saw it was in small, square boxes in the frozen food section. I still have flashbacks to those days when I caught sight of the spinach box wedged into our tiny freezer. I had to move to America to learn that spinach was a cute, rather pretty green leaf that you could eat raw and call salad. Altogether a better option, I say.

My love affair with spinach really began the day I tasted Creamed Spinach at Daniel's Broiler in Seattle, Washington. These days I easily get through 4 lbs. every week – mostly in smoothies, but also creamed, crammed into a large baking dish, and baked in the oven (recipe at www.carriebrown.com). Here's another delicious, refreshing way to get your spinach fix.

Don't eat the oranges unless you're at goal and know oranges don't make your blood sugar crazy.

Lettuce Soup

Prep: 10 mins | Cook: 60 mins | Total: 1 hr. 10 mins

2 oz. / 55g butter **SUB: ghee for dairy-free**

12 oz. / 335g (approx.2 heads) Romaine lettuce leaves

4oz. / 110g green (spring) onions / scallions

3 cups / 1 ½ pints chicken stock

½ cup / 4 fl oz. thick coconut milk

½ tsp. sea salt

2 tsp. lemon juice

3 tsp. onion powder

2 oz. / 55g fresh spinach

½ tsp. konjac flour (glucomannan power)

½ tsp. guar gum

Heat the butter in a large pan or stick pot over medium heat and sauté the lettuce and onions until soft.

Add the stock and simmer for 45 minutes.

Transfer the stock and lettuce to the blender, add the coconut milk, sea salt, lemon juice, and onion powder, and blend on high until very smooth.

Add the spinach and blend just until it disappears.

Turn the blender to low, and slowly tap the konjac flour, then the guar gum through the opening in the lid. Blend for 5 seconds.

~~~~~~

Wait. I know what you're thinking. Lettuce made into soup? Smooth, warm lettuce? Are you kidding me right now?

Well I don't know about you, but sometimes I just get tired of chomping through bags of lettuce, spinach, and other leafy, salady stuff; but I still want to get my greens in. What better way than to turn it into something warm, and satisfying, and delicious? Enter Lettuce Soup. The other upside? You can eat way more greens when they're pulverized into a liquid, so if you're struggling to consume enough green stuff in a day, soup it!

Cheesy Biscuits / Scones

Prep: 10 mins | Cook: 10 mins | Total: 20 mins
Makes: 8 – 10

9 oz. / 250g almond flour / ground almonds (NOT almond meal)

½ tsp. salt

4 tsp. baking powder

1 tsp. xanthan gum

2 oz. / 55g butter

2 oz. / 55g sharp (strong) cheddar cheese, finely grated

⅓ cup / 2 ½ fl oz. unsweetened coconut or unsweetened almond milk

1 beaten egg to glaze

Heat oven to 400ºF.

Put the almond flour, other dry ingredients and butter in a food processor and pulse until it resembles fine breadcrumbs. You can also do this by hand if that's your thing.

Turn into a bowl and mix in the cheese until evenly distributed. Make a well in the center of the dry ingredients and pour in the milk.

Mix by hand to form a dough. It will be a little sticky.

Using almond flour to dust the surface, knead the dough lightly until smooth.

Roll out the dough to ¾ inch thick.

Cut out biscuits using a round or fluted cutter.

Gather up the trimmings into a ball, re-roll and cut remaining dough into rounds.

Place the scones on a baking sheet.

Brush tops with a beaten egg.

Bake for 8 – 10 minutes until golden brown.

~~~~~~

Oh, for the love of all things cheesy and delicious, I love these Cheesy Biscuits almost more than life itself. I promise you won't believe they have no flour in. Grain- and gluten-free peeps rejoice! Just 10 minutes to throw together and a swift 10 minutes in the oven. Heaven awaits.

Sour Cream and Chive Biscuits / Scones

Prep: 10 mins | Cook: 15 mins | Total: 25 mins
Makes: 12

15 oz. / 420g almond flour / ground almonds (NOT almond meal)

4 tsp. baking powder

1 tsp. baking soda

2 tsp. xanthan gum

½ tsp. salt

6 oz. / 170g unsalted butter, cold

1 egg

½ cup full-fat sour cream

1 TBSP cold water

½ oz. fresh chives, chopped

6 oz. / 170g full-fat feta cheese, chopped into small pieces

Beaten egg to glaze

Paprika

Pre-heat oven to 375ºF. Place almond flour, baking powder, baking soda, xanthan gum, salt and cold butter into a food processor and pulse just until it resembles breadcrumbs. Do not over process!

Turn into a mixing bowl and add the egg, sour cream, water, chives and feta cheese, and mix just enough to form a rough, soft dough. Turn onto a board and knead about 10 times until the dough comes together. It will be shaggy.

Flatten the dough lightly with your hand until it is a 1 inch thick square. Cut into 2 inch squares with a sharp knife.

Place biscuits on a baking sheet, brush with beaten egg and sprinkle with paprika.

Bake in the center of the oven for 12 – 15 minutes until golden brown.

~~~~~~

Top Tip: Beware buying ready-crumbled feta cheese – it has corn or other starches in it to prevent the crumbles caking together. Instead, buy a piece of feta cheese and chop into small pieces. Depending on your goals and where you are on your journey, if you want or need to reduce the fat, you can use low-fat versions of sour cream and feta.

Tomato Basil Biscuits / Scones

Prep: 10 mins | Cook: 10 mins | Total: 20 mins
Makes: 8

9 oz. / 250g almond flour / ground almonds (NOT almond meal)

½ tsp. salt

4 tsp. baking powder

1 tsp. xanthan gum

3 tsp. dried basil

2 oz. / 55g butter **SUB: ghee for dairy-free**

2 oz. / 55g sun-dried tomatoes, pre-soaked in hot water to soften, drained, and then chopped

⅓ cup / 2 ½ fl oz. unsweetened coconut or unsweetened almond milk

Beaten egg to glaze

Heat oven to 400ºF.

Put the almond flour, other dry ingredients, basil and butter in a food processor and pulse until it resembles fine breadcrumbs. You can also do this by hand if that's your thing.

Turn into a bowl and mix in the sun-dried tomatoes until evenly distributed.

Make a well in the center of the dry ingredients and pour in the milk.

Mix by hand to form a dough. Knead the dough lightly until smooth.

Divide dough into eight 2 oz. / 55g pieces of dough.

Roll each piece in your hands to make a ball, please on baking sheet and flatten gently to resemble a cookie.

Brush tops with beaten egg.

Bake for 10 minutes until golden brown.

Carefully use a serrated knife to cut open, especially if they are still warm, as they are quite fragile.

~~~~~~

If you like tomatoes, these biscuits will send you into a complete dither. In a good way.

www.carriebrown.com

KONJAC FLOUR: WHAT, WHY, HOW

Konjac flour – also known as glucomannan powder – is hands-down the best thickener in a KETO kitchen, and especially when it comes to cooking soups, konjac is simply magical.

Follow the recipes and only use konjac flour / glucomannan powder as your thickener. DO NOT try and swap it out with guar or xanthan gum (unless you want a sad soup). There is no other successful KETO sub for konjac. Please avail yourself of some and prepare to be amazed!

Guar and xanthan gums have a different purpose and you will not get the best result if you use them. They have a tendency to become slimy, and do not hold up as well under extremely long cooking times. Guar gum, particularly, loses its thickening abilities in the presence of too much or too long heating. Guar also fails if it is cooked with things that are too acidic or too alkaline.

Here's some good things to know about konjac flour:

- Konjac does not get slimy and is completely tasteless.
- Konjac does not break down or "leak" when heated for a long time.
- Konjac thickens very evenly.
- Konjac is very easy to use, and since it takes a little time to fully thicken it does not clump the instant it is introduced into a liquid.
- Since konjac doesn't clump instantly it is much less stressful and more successful to use than gums. I love it when you're successful in the kitchen!
- When konjac is used in a sauce, gravy or other liquid, it reheats perfectly the next day. It regains the exact same texture and consistency that it had when you first made it, whether you reheat it in the microwave or on the stovetop. Gums, not so much.
- Dishes made with konjac also freeze, defrost and reheat perfectly.
- Konjac is an emulsifier as well as a thickener, so it has the ability to help prevent curdling and separating. This is very good. Curdling is very bad.
- Konjac has about 10x the thickening power of cornstarch (cornflour).
- You use a very small amount of konjac flour, so that pricey tub lasts a very long time.

Here's some tips and tricks when using konjac flour:

- Always use a measuring spoon rather than guessing. Konjac is very strong and you can easily add too much if you don't measure.
- While stirring your sauce or liquids with one hand, gently tap the measuring spoon containing the konjac on the side of the bowl or pan. Alternatively you can sprinkle the konjac evenly over the surface of the liquid and stir rapidly.
- Once you've added the amount in the recipe, if it does not seem thick enough, wait a few minutes to allow the konjac to fully thicken.

More info and where-to-buy konjac here: *www.carriebrown.com/archives/23109*

KETOVANGELIST KITCHEN RESOURCES

WEBSITE : www.ketovangelistkitchen.com

PODCAST : www.ketovangelistkitchen.com/category/podcast

FACEBOOK GROUP : www.facebook.com/groups/ketovangelistkitchen

TWITTER : www.twitter.com/KetovanKitchen

PINTEREST : www.pinterest.com/KetovanKitchen

INSTAGRAM : www.instagram.com/ketovangelistkitchen

KETOVANGELIST GENERAL KETO RESOURCES

WEBSITE : www.ketovangelistkitchen.com

PODCAST : www.ketovangelist.com/category/podcast/

FACEBOOK GROUP : www.facebook.com/groups/theketogenicathlete/

KETOGENIC ATHLETE RESOURCES

WEBSITE : www.theketogenicathlete.com

PODCAST : www.theketogenicathlete.com/category/podcast/

FACEBOOK GROUP : www.facebook.com/groups/theketogenicathlete/

www.carriebrown.com

WHERE TO FIND ME

www.CarrieBrown.com : delicious recipes for optimal nutrition, wellness, & fat-loss, with tips & tricks for living a super healthy, sane life, as well as travel & things to make you think.

PODCAST : www.ketovangelistkitchen.com/category/podcast

FACEBOOK (page) : www.facebook.com/CarrieBrownBlog

FACEBOOK (personal) : www.facebook.com/flamingavocado

TWITTER : www.twitter.com/CarrieBrownBlog

PINTEREST : www.pinterest.com/CarrieBrownBlog

INSTAGRAM
@carrieontrippin : day-to-day moments captured with my iPhone
@biggirlcamera : road trips, landscapes, flowers, fences, barns, & whatever else grabs my attention captured with my Big Girl Camera
@lifeinthesanelane : food, recipes, inspiration, and sane living tips
@mistermchenry : The world according to Mr. McHenry

FLICKR : www.flickr.com/photos/carrieontrippin

MEDIUM : www.medium.com/@CarrieBrownBlog : random musings on life, the Universe, & everything. Possibly rantier, more sensitive, & more controversial.

COOKBOOKS

E-cookbook / pdf versions : www.carriebrown.com/archives/31768

Print versions : www.amazon.com/author/browncarrie

www.carriebrown.com

I am an author, podcast co-host, recipe developer, and photographer, creating useful, fun, and beautiful stuff about food, travel, and living a healthy, unmedicated, and sane life.

I use my ex-professional pastry chef talents to create scrumptious recipes to help the world eat smarter, live better, and put the 'healthy' back into healthy again. I create gluten-, grain-, sugar-, soy-free recipes for KETO, LCHF, LowCarb, Paleo, Primal, WheatBelly, Wild Diet, SANE, and other health-focused dietary approaches using real foods. What a concept! Healthy can be more delicious than you ever imagined.

This book joins The KETO Ice Cream Scoop, The KETO Crockpot, KETO for the Holidays, 101 KETO Beverages, and Eat Smarter! Smoothies and Sides on the culinary bookshelf.

When I am not creating tasty things for you to eat and drink, I hurtle around the country creating images of all the awesomeness there is out there. Which is a lot. Also, I like life better when it's real, rambunctious, and slightly irreverent.

I love the color yellow, talk funny, and adore people who are kind to others in spite of their own pain. I think fences can teach us many things about life, and perspective changes everything. I don't care for crab, but duck will get me all kinds of excited.

I love living in Seattle with an abundance of clematis, an alarming amount of coconut oil, and the Ketogenic world's most popular team of cats – Zebedee, Daisy, and Mr. McHenry. (RIP Chiko, Dougal, Penelope, and Florence). We have a boatload of fun.

www.carriebrown.com

MAIN COURSE SOUPS

Recipe	Page
All That Mac & Cheese Soup	71*
Bacon and Brussels Sprouts Chowder	23
Bacon BBQ Chicken Soup	53
Baconated French Onion Soup	65
Beef Barlesque Stew	55
Chicken and Dumplings Stew	69
Chicken and Mushroom Soup Uncanned	29
Chicken Noodle Soup	51
Chicken Tortilla Soup	47
Chilled Avocado Cream with Prawns	49
Clam Chowder	37
Drunken Duck Gumbo	63
Is It or Isn't It Chili	73
Lasagna Soup	25
Loaded Baked Notato Soup	67
MadLove Burger Bowl	57
Prawn Cocktail Gazpacho	33*
Roasted Pepper and Smoked Sausage Soup	43
Salmon and Leek Chowder	27
Sausage and Kale Soup	31

Sausage, Fennel and Leek Hodgepodge...............................45

Smoky Turkey Hazelnut Soup 61

Thai Chicken Coconut Soup 35

The Ham's In A Pickle Hodgepodge...............................59

Turkey Pot Pie Gumbo 39

Wild Chicken and Rice Soup.......................................41*

BYO (BUILD YOUR OWN) SOUPS

All In A Pickle Soup...77

Avocado Gazpacho...78

Broccoli Cheddar Soup 93*

Cauliflower Cheese Soup...89*

Confetti Veggie Soup 88

Cream of Celery Soup 96

Cream of Mushroom Soup..90

Creamed Onion Soup 99

Creamy Broccolini Soup..91

Creamy Cucumber Soup 79

Cucumber, Celery and Dill Soup..................................84

Cuke and Cauli Soup 83

Green Bean Casserole Soup..97

Green Pepper Leek Soup 86

Leek and Cauliflower Soup 85

Lemon Veggie Cream Soup 84

Lettuce Soup 102

Parsley Cream Soup 100

Rosemary Asparagus Soup 92

Spiced Cauliflower Soup 87

Spiced Pumpkin Soup 95

Spinach and Orange Soup 101

Tomato Salad Soup 81

Tomato Times Two Soup 82

Cheesy Biscuits 103*

Sour Cream and Chive Biscuits 105*

Tomato Basil Biscuits 106

Ketovangelist Resources 108

Konjac Flour: What, Why, How 107

Ingredients and Equipment Resources: 5

Serving Sizes and Macronutrients 21

(*NOT dairy free)

Printed in Poland
by Amazon Fulfillment
Poland Sp. z o.o., Wrocław